# NIGHT SEA JOURNEYING

"This deeply insightful book stresses the recovery potential of exploring the spiritual dimension when dealing with psychological trauma. The evocative night sea journey metaphor perfectly captures how emotionally deprived and abused children can heal and grow through facing their inner turmoil. Using vivid case histories, plus a rich interpretation of New Testament texts, combined with masterly advice from the likes of Carl Jung and Thomas Merton, Gardner proves herself a rare and valuable guide."

—LARRY CULLIFORD,
author of *The Psychology of Spirituality*

"Fiona's book is a powerful, unsentimental exploration of trauma's impact on the soul. Through poetic storytelling, gospel imagery, and sea metaphors, she guides readers from brokenness to restoration. Her vignettes reveal Christ's radical love for the traumatized while blending insights from psychotherapy and spiritual direction. Muscular yet grace-filled, this work offers professional, personal, and spiritual wisdom, summoning the authentic, God-given self in those shaped by relational trauma."

—BELINDA WEST,
Psychoanalytic Psychotherapist, London

"To read Fiona Gardner's *Night Sea Journeying: Soul Recovery from Childhood Trauma* is to be touched. Gardner writes with rare compassion and profound wisdom. Drawing from Jung, Merton, and decades of clinical insight, Gardner accompanies survivors into the hidden depths of their own souls, revealing that even after devastation, the divine inner other transforms trauma, illuminating its darkness. Soul recovery unfolds as Gardner tenderly invites the survivor to enter and experience a very sacred journey."

—STEPHANIE AREL,
Lecturer, Fordham University, New York

"Fiona Gardner's *Night Sea Journeying* is a wonderful book which explores trauma and abuse in infancy, childhood, and adolescence, and the potential for recovery. Drawing upon her experience as a spiritual director as well as her knowledge of theology and analytical psychology, she describes the process of reuniting parts of ourselves that may be hidden or in exile. Significant insights emerge not only through her knowledge of Carl Jung and Thomas Merton, but especially through her inclusion of the stories of clients that describe their own journeys toward wholeness."

—ED SELLNER,
Professor Emeritus of Theology and Spirituality,
St. Catherine University, Minnesota

# NIGHT SEA JOURNEYING

*Soul recovery from childhood trauma*

FIONA GARDNER

CASCADE *Books* • Eugene, Oregon

NIGHT SEA JOURNEYING
Soul Recovery from Childhood Trauma



Cascade Books
An Imprint of Wipf and Stock Publishers
199 W. 8th Ave., Suite 3
Eugene, OR 97401

www.wipfandstock.com

PAPERBACK ISBN: 979-8-3852-2783-9
HARDCOVER ISBN: 979-8-3852-2784-6
EBOOK ISBN: 979-8-3852-2785-3

*Cataloguing-in-Publication data:*

Names: Gardner, Fiona, author.

Title: Night sea journeying : soul recovery from childhood trauma / Fiona Gardner.

Description: Eugene, OR: Cascade Books, 2025 | Includes bibliographical references and index.

Identifiers: ISBN 979-8-3852-2783-9 (paperback) | ISBN 979-8-3852-2784-6 (hardcover) | ISBN 979-8-3852-2785-3 (ebook)

Subjects: LCSH: Psychology, Religious. | Post-traumatic stress disorder. | Carl Jung, 1875–1961. | Thomas Merton, 1915–1968.

Classification: BL53 G37 2025 (paperback) | BL53 (ebook)

VERSION NUMBER 12/05/25

For Lindsey, Elira, Harrison, and Callum

Go down
into the plans of God.
Go down
deep as you may.
Fear not
for your fragility
under that weight of water.
Fear not
for life or limb.
sharks attack savagely.
Fear not
the power of treacherous currents under the sea.
Simply, do not be afraid.
Let go.
You will be led . . .

Dom Helder Camara, "The Desert is Fertile"

# Contents

# Acknowledgments

Thank you to Reverend Catherine Williams from the Spiritual Direction Forum UK, for her support of an earlier draft of this book.

I am very grateful to the artist Robin Baring for his kind permission to use his oil painting entitled *Night Sea Journeying* as the cover illustration.

I would like to thank all those whom I have seen both in my psychotherapy work and for spiritual direction over the years, who have contributed to my understanding of trauma. Similarly for my own experience in two analyses with analytical psychologists, and in spiritual direction.

Grateful thanks to Leila Smith of The Yoga Studio for introducing me to the breathwork and practice of Sandra Sabatini.

Thank you to my family, especially to my husband, Peter, for their support, interest, and love.

We stand on the shoulders of giants; the work of two inspirational people has greatly influenced my work and writing. The first is the analytical psychologist Carl Jung; the second the Trappist monk and writer Thomas Merton. A deep debt is acknowledged to both.

# 1

# Introduction to the Journey

"I had to recognize and accept that my soul is a child and that my God in my soul is a child."[1]

THIS EXTRAORDINARY STATEMENT FROM the analytical psychologist Carl Jung came to him during his own night sea journeying, an exploration to re-find his soul. If, as he suggests, our soul is a divine child, then what happens to our soul when we have been traumatized and abused in childhood? This book is an exploration of both the damage that is done and the soul recovery that can happen, if we allow it. The suggestion is that while therapeutic help is important, spiritual change and awakening is essential. This is a book about finding oneself at the deepest dimension, about the process of becoming free from the limitations that a traumatic past has imposed on our personal sense of self. It is about finding our true purpose in life, and how childhood trauma once integrated can feed into this purpose.

We all have our personal life stories formed from the environment we were born into, and the particular circumstances of our infancy and childhood. This shapes a script that partially defines us, and, how we perceive ourselves to be—our sense of self. That same sense of self can determine how we experience events,

1. Jung, *Red Book*, 244.

and how much we identify with this conditioned mind. For some of us this sense of self can be deeply problematic, and so we carry a sadness from our past into our present life. However, this is not all that we are, and the heavy burden of childhood trauma can be integrated, leaving a space and potential for the true self—the soul to emerge from its hiding place.

## THE SOUL—WHAT IS IT?

While Jung, from his explorations in the unconscious, experienced his soul as a divine child, generally defining the soul is something that both theologians and psychoanalysts have struggled with, to the extent of sometimes displaying reluctance in even using the word. The etymology of the word *soul* links to the Latin word *anima*, and anima links to the Greek word *psyche*. However, some have distinguished the soul from the psyche as conceptually different; and the words *soul* and *psyche* are used in different contexts.

A general definition of soul is that it is the immaterial essence and animating principle of a person's life. There is a deeply personal essence within each one of us, and in all of created life too. The soul the vital spark, the imperishable personal spirit, the principle of life that enlivens us; it is the source of everything in us that is alive. Wherever there is any manifestation of life, then there is a manifestation of soul. Jung, who has been called by the Jungian Anne Baring one of "the great astronauts of the soul," extended and deepened the definition out from only the personal, and "in his writings and his practice, soul becomes not so much something that belongs to us as something to which we belong—a vast and unexplored dimension of reality . . . connection with the transcendent."[2]

Jung framed the soul as the sacred dimension, a divine spark, essential to human life. He described it as a hidden treasure, a treasure hard to attain and like a shining pearl. Donald Kalsched, a contemporary Jungian, writes that the soul, sometimes

2. Baring, *Dream of the Cosmos*, 244–45.

encapsulated in the image of a divine child, does not belong entirely to this world. And neither do we. Kalsched sees the human soul as, always, a creature of both worlds: divine and human, time-bound and eternal, mortal and immortal. "Straddling these two worlds, the soul is the seat of our dual destiny and home to what Shakespeare called our 'immortal longings.' It is also home to what Jung called 'our religious instinct.'"[3]

Amongst the psychoanalysts, Donald Winnicott, the pediatrician and child and adult psychoanalyst, referred to a sacred incommunicado center of the personality. He also called this mystery the true self, which he says cannot be defined, except to say that it "collects together the details of the experience of aliveness."[4] He saw the soul as our true self, a sense of self based on authentic experience, and the feeling of being truly present and alive. It means that one can be spontaneous and open to what is happening, so aware and awake. It's the part of us that is creative and feels real.

Winnicott wrote about how as we grow and develop the true self (if it has not been seriously interrupted), it results in what he described as a strengthening of the sense of being real. Winnicott formulated the idea of the true self in response to his thinking about what he called the false self or the compliant self, which makes us feel increasingly unreal and leads to a sense of futility. Other analysts have referred to the soul in terms like the lost heart of the self, and the lifegiver. Here the soul is about a vitality, an aliveness and power that is stronger than the conditioned mind, and, given space, stronger than the traumatized mind: it is an essence within us, but that also transcends what and who one is as a person by connecting us to all of creation.

In theology there are a variety of definitions where the soul is seen as basically our mind, or our emotions, and/or our will. The soul is further defined as the part of us that connects with divinity, a secret dwelling where God abides, where we meet with God. In the Magnificat, Mary's joyful song begins: "My soul glorifies the

3. Kalsched, *Trauma and the Soul*, 16.

4. Winnicott, *Maturational Processes*, 148.

Lord and my spirit rejoices in God my Savior."[5] One perspective on this is that the soul is a channel for us to experience God in our spirit, where the body is the outer level, and our connection to God paved through the soul. In the Magnificat, God's power and grace is magnified through the soul, and then experienced fully in the deepest core of the inner spirit. The soul is often believed to survive the death of our body, and the ultimate purpose of faith is often seen as the salvation of our souls.

Thomas Merton, the Trappist monk and writer, experienced God as the center of his soul. The soul was therefore "a spiritual sanctuary," a place of secrecy reached by silence and solitude and isolation. For Merton, God's grace works in the soul of a person:

> The most beautiful thing about it is to see how the desires of the soul inspired by God so fit in and harmonize with grace that holy things seem *natural* to the soul, seem to be part of its very self. That is what God wants to create in us—that marvellously simple spontaneity in which His life becomes perfectly ours and our life His, and it seems absolutely inborn in us to act as His children, and to have His light shining in our eyes.[6]

Here Merton the monk can be seen to agree with both the psychoanalysts and Jungian analytical psychologists, when he describes the divine interaction and spiritual development of the soul as a fount for spontaneity, and as the foundation of the true self, acting as God's children in union with God.

## WHAT IS CHILDHOOD TRAUMA?

Lord my God, I call for help by day;
I cry at night before you. . . .
For my soul is filled with evils;
my life is on the brink of the grave,
I am reckoned as one in the tomb;

5. Luke 1:46–47.
6. Merton, *Entering the Silence*, 74–75, 243.

I have reached the end of my strength. [7]

Thomas Merton describes how at the age of six he learned about his mother's terminal illness.

> Then one day father gave me a note to read . . . My mother was informing me, by mail, that she was about to die, and would never see me again.
>
> I took the note out under the maple tree in the back yard, and worked over it, until I had made it all out, and had gathered what it really meant. And a tremendous weight of sadness and depression settled on me. It was not the grief of a child, with pangs of sorrow and many tears. It had something of the heavy perplexity and gloom of adult grief, and was therefore all the more of a burden because, it was, to that extent, unnatural. I suppose one reason for this was that I had more or less to arrive at the truth by induction.[8]

Trauma, sometimes referred to as adverse childhood experiences, describes highly stressful and damaging events or situations that occur during infancy, childhood, and/or adolescence. These can be a single event, or cumulative experiences, that damage the child emotionally and developmentally, and that have been linked to later mental and physical health. Trauma is primarily an injury to the capacity to feel—to feel connected to others, and, to one's body.

All our experiences in infancy and childhood have a huge impact on how we grow and develop—our thoughts, feelings, and the way we relate to others and behave. Adult well-being is strongly linked to the attachment relationships we had as a child, and to any interruptions, impingements, or damage to these. In this book, the word *trauma* is used as it so well conveys the rupture in the child's sense of self and the previous way of being. Trauma is an experience that is unbearable, in the sense that it overwhelms the usual

7. Psalm 88:1–4, as rendered in Johnson, ed., *Benedictine Daily Prayer*, 1161.

8. Merton, *Seven Storey Mountain*, 24.

defensive structures that can protect us as we develop. There can be a single shattering incident, or a long run of unmet dependency needs that mount up as cumulative trauma. Winnicott called such acute deprivations primitive agonies, which are by their nature unthinkable; they cannot be assimilated by thinking about them, and for many children the capacity to even begin to understand what is happening or has happened is impossible.

For some people the very idea that childhood can be meaningfully associated with joy, and so in any meaningful way carefree, is unrealistic. A significant number of children have experiences of emotional, physical, and sexual abuse, and others are neglected. Some may have experienced a restrictive illness or disability, or been exposed to loss or upsetting situations by the adults in their lives, or by friends or siblings. A difficult or damaged childhood will cast a long shadow, and can lead to an inability to trust and problems in later relationships. The lack of trust can lead to a sense of reluctance to relinquish any control with others, and so in the context of religious experience it can mean it is hard to accept simplicity and dependence in any relationship with God. For the child who feels unacceptable and has been treated in an unacceptable way, it can be hard to believe that they are fundamentally good.

"Soul murder" is a term probably first coined in the nineteenth century, and used by the playwrights Henrik Ibsen and August Strindberg. Ibsen defined it as the destruction of the love of life in another person. His character speaks:

> You have committed the one mortal sin! . . . You have killed the love of life in me. Do you understand what that means? The Bible speaks of a mysterious sin for which there is no forgiveness. I have never understood what it could be; but now I understand. The great unpardonable sin is to murder the love of life in a human soul . . . You have killed all the joy of life in me.[9]

The analyst Leonard Shengold, who wrote two books on soul murder, uses the term to describe the willful abuse and neglect of

9. Ibsen, *John Gabriel Borkman*, 331.

children by adults that are of sufficient intensity and frequency to be traumatic; and so the child's emotional development and soul development is profoundly and negatively affected, so much so that the soul may go into hiding, a form of soul protection.[10]

What is the soul protecting itself from? The development of the soul in infancy and early childhood depends on a reasonably empathic environment, where there is a sense of the soul safely indwelling the body. This empathy establishes a pattern whereby the mother or mothering person introduces and reintroduces the baby's mind and body to each other. The gradual development means the small baby becomes a whole person with psychosomatic unity, who embodies in their very center a vital spark. Trauma, especially emotional trauma, interrupts the normal processes by which the true embodied self comes into being. That of God, the divine spark and sense of spontaneous aliveness within, becomes cut off and exiled, or deeply hidden, to protect the soul from further damage.

The unfortunate implication of trauma—especially if it occurs in early infancy—is that it often introduces a lifetime of symptomatology that often includes a feeling of free-floating anxiety or unnameable dread that becomes associated with the threatened falling apart of any sense of a coherent self. It is this dread that has a life of its own, as in order to protect the psyche and soul from re-experiencing the unbearable, further defenses are formed, and it is often these that become symptoms in their own right, and that can start to dominate. The defenses are then both life-saving and life-denying. In the development of the child who has been traumatized, one part of the child's psyche stays regressed, stuck in the trauma, and another part too rapidly progresses by growing up too fast, often functioning as a false self that then caretakes the authentic soul part and tries to cope with the world.

In this way trauma is imprisoning, limiting life, and making its presence felt by the variety of symptoms, disorders and behaviors that protect the child and later the adult from re-experiencing and so integrating the trauma. It is these protective defenses that can accompany us long into adulthood, screening all relations

10. See Shengold, *Soul Murder Revisited.*

with the outside world, so that spontaneity and creativity become difficult. Each new life event is potentially a threat to being retraumatized, as the caretaking self is unable to assess realistic danger, but is instead hypervigilant to avoid any repetition. Paradoxically there is at the same time a pull towards familiar scenarios and familiar dangers, while dreams or rather nightmares are often peopled by persecutory figures. This is famously called repetition compulsion.[11]

## LOSING ONE'S SOUL

Following trauma, the soul mostly goes into exile. The mind can remain occupied by the perpetrator or by the traumatic situation, so life continues, but with part of the person absent—not present to the present, but in some part of the mind still alert to any recurring trauma. Always vigilant, keeping watch, ready to respond in fear and anticipation of what might happen next. Trauma obscures our spirituality—it changes the way that we can trust or have faith in ourselves, other people, and in God. Our true spiritual soul self is hidden. Here's what Joe says about his soul—Joe is someone whose night sea journeying we follow through this book:

> If you'd asked me about my soul when I was in my twenties or even in my thirties, I wouldn't have known what you were talking about . . . not sure I would have had much clue about my inner life either. I was too intent in pretending to be something I wasn't. Of course, I see now that I wasn't coping—but the way I chose to "cope" was to try to change how I looked, to try and get bigger and stronger. It began okay, but then I got hooked into trying to be different—anybody but me. I used to spend hours trying to toughen up, looking in magazines to see how to develop my muscles. It turned out it wasn't a great way of living, but it was what I did at the time—until it all fell apart, and then I had to confront everything that had happened when I was a small kid.

11. Freud, *Beyond the Pleasure Principle XVIII*, 36–38.

> So, as a young adult if I'd had a soul I wouldn't have known or cared . . . Now I can see that a huge part of me had just gone AWOL—nobody was home, I was just more or less existing. I eventually managed to get a steady job in social care, but all the time with this great fog that had descended on me, that stopped me feeling anything much at all.

As adults, we might lose our soul when too busy and involved in the realities of everyday living and working. There may be no time or space to reflect and consider. Or, we might deny that we even have a soul, and take no interest in our inner world and spiritual well-being. Thomas Merton, early in his conversion and before joining the Abbey of Gethsemani as a Trappist monk, was wrestling with what the soul was and wrote down in his notebook some of the thoughts from St. Bonaventure about how the soul "distracted as it is by worries . . . clouded by images . . . torn by disordered desires" is then separated from "itself as the image of God."[12]

Losing the soul, then, is about losing the connection between what we know of ourselves, and the vast unknown and unknowable. This is the connection between the conscious and the unconscious, and between ourselves and God—whether personalized by Christ, or, as in another spiritual context, by Buddha nature. The soul can be seen as a thread—a golden thread or the connecting ribbon. Without it we become alienated not only from the essence of ourselves, but also from the original oneness and from the experience of divine radiance.

## WHAT IS NIGHT SEA JOURNEYING?

This is a universal myth with cultural variations. The essence of the myth is about a hero who when traveling across the sea is devoured by a water-monster. With the hero inside, the huge fish swims from the West to the East. The hero lights a fire in the belly of the monster and, feeling hungry, cuts a piece of the heart. Soon

12. Merton, *Run to the Mountain*, 321.

afterwards, the hero notices that the fish has glided onto dry land; cutting open the monster from within, the hero slips out. As individual freedom is regained, so the hero may at the same time free all those who were previously devoured by the monster, and who now slip out too. The night sea journey has been represented in other ways, including being swallowed by a dragon, by imprisonment or crucifixion, or abduction, being oppressed and overwhelmed, and by the difficulty in getting free from such powers. In the language of the mystics, it is the dark night of the soul. The symbolism involves ever present death alongside the hope of survival and rebirth. The setting of the sea traditionally represents the unconscious, which is unpredictable, dangerous: a place of chaos.

Psychologically and spiritually, taking the night sea journey is about a process of reuniting parts of ourselves that may be in hiding or in exile, and that we have kept pushed away from our consciousness in order to be able to get on with our lives as best we can. In the context of this book, night sea journeying is about reuniting with our soul—the true self part of ourselves that was lost because of childhood trauma. To do this the past trauma of childhood has to be acknowledged, recognized, and integrated—it's about a coming to terms not only with what happened, but also a recognition of what has been lost. Such a journey involves deep diving into the unconscious "to the land of ghosts somewhere beyond this world," a descent into the unknown that Jung called the archetypal myth of the night sea journey.[13]

A myth like this is not to be taken literally, but offers a generic framework for understanding and for taking us out of the familiar into the unknown. Coming to terms with past trauma is not easy—it is complex, complicated, and multilayered. For survivors the journey is both to save oneself, and so in doing this saving the world, because the attempts to overcome and shed light on what has been felt as personal darkness will also help others. This is because it reduces the power of those who perpetrate, and beyond that lessens the power of collective darkness. Joseph Campbell writes:

13. Jung, *Practice of Psychotherapy*, para. 455.

> We have not even to risk the adventure alone, for the heroes of all time have gone before us. The labyrinth is thoroughly known; we have only to follow the thread of the hero path. And where we had thought to find an abomination, we shall find a god. And where we had thought to slay another, we shall slay ourselves. And where we had thought to travel outward, we shall come to the center of our own existence. And where we had thought to be alone, we shall be with all the world.[14]

Where the journey of the survivor of trauma *differs* from that of the hero journey is that the hero leaves the realm of light and certainty to travel into darkness, whereas the person who was traumatized as a child has been living since the trauma in a secret twilight and ambiguous world—neither light nor dark. The traumatized person has been getting through, but is still in captivity to the aftereffects of what happened, and so spiritually numbed or deadened. Where the hero journey and the journey of the trauma survivor *is* similar is that both require a death and resurrection. Both are about leaving one condition and finding the source of life to bring forth a freedom, and a more mature, less restricted condition that expresses a truth about the person's life. This might be called individuation; it might be called redemption, but it is essentially soul recovery—recovery of the spirit of life and hope. Edward Sellner writes:

> It can become a pilgrimage toward greater freedom and wholeness when we are given the courage to face the terror of the unknown and to persist, despite all those parts of ourselves, all those relationships . . . that seem to want us to stay the way we were.[15]

The journey that takes the person from the aftereffects of trauma through to the possibility of feeling their spirituality is an exodus through darkness into the unknown and out into the dawn of a brighter place—night sea journeying. Here's the account of Evie, parts of whose journeying are also included in the book:

14. Campbell, "Power of Myth, 'The Hero's Journey.'"
15. Sellner, *Soul-Making*, 4.

I don't think I thought about my soul until much later . . . I did go to Sunday school as a child, but that seemed to be about trying to be good all the time, and helping other people. I remember learning by heart the order of the books of the Bible and getting a prize for reciting it. But that was all an extension of home and so more of the same—except people were kind, I do remember that. But it was part of the same feeling of being shut in . . . and I now see being shut off.

I've always been a sucker for videos of animals who have been held in captivity for years—perhaps in some grim zoo or a bear bile farm in Asia where you see that they are barely alive—just going through the motions—eating, sleeping, half alive . . . then they are rescued, and the film shows them being let out of their cage, sniffing fresh air and for the first time *ever* walking on the earth, feeling grass. Well, some of them leave, but others stay in the cage—too frightened at first—but then they are encouraged out. Freed finally from cruelty and from cramped conditions, and turning to the huge sky in wonder and joy. Then . . . I cry . . . and donate some money as it's clearly resonating deeply within me . . . I've never been kept in that sort of captivity or subjected to that sort of cruelty, but I have been caught up—or tied up—in the past. It's a bit like being occupied by someone or something else—yes, a state of occupation, and it leaves me in so many ways searching to be free and fully alive. But free from what—nothing extraordinary or sensational, but free from never feeling good enough, or loveable, or being able to trust . . . or, and this is painful to say, feeling free to be joyful. It's a longing to be really alive, and to know something more than what happened when I was a child.

What I want to describe are some of the times when the searching has got me somewhere, or I've had a bit of a breakthrough into awareness. These are times when the bonds begin to loosen and even fall away—but it's mostly been so slow, so perhaps it's only when looking back that I can think yes, I was out of the cage and then ran back, or, yes, I *did* feel the grass and *see* the sky, and knowing

> there is something more I took steps out into the wider world and breathed deeply.

Clearly neither Evie or Joe speak for all traumatized children, as everyone traumatized as a child has a different and unique story, but their experiences may speak to some of the universal themes and struggles that can take place in soul recovery. Both Evie and Joe are drawn from personal and professional experience. As children both Evie and Joe had cumulative trauma, as adults both struggled with coming to terms with what had happened to them, and both gradually integrated the past enough to feel sufficiently emotionally stable to find their specific spiritual path.

## THE STRUCTURE OF THIS BOOK

This book is divided into three parts. The first part, chapters 2 and 3, is about before starting the night sea journey. The focus for chapter 2 is to look further at what it means for the soul to be hidden and damaged, with a deeper discussion on the effects of trauma and cumulative trauma on the development of the soul in childhood. The first part of chapter 3 is about specific defensive self-care systems that tend to get established following trauma in childhood, and how this leads to a "stuck" place, reducing the possibility of feeling fully spiritually alive in the world as an adult. In the second part of this chapter, the longing for things to be different can be triggered by fear and panic, and as the defenses become more problematic and may even break down, there is a deep yearning for healing and cleansing, and this longing is explored in the context of Jesus' baptism in Mark's Gospel, and our need to become more truly ourself.

Part 2 is the night sea journey—the heart of the book. Chapters 4 through 7 follow what can happen when, as an adult, the person reaches the insight that something has to change and embarks on a journey of discovery. Chapter 4 is about approaching the seashore from dry land. The Gospel of Mark is used in these chapters to complement the myth of the night sea journey, both as one way of understanding the spiritual desire for something to change, and also interpreting what happens. In Mark's Gospel, the seashore becomes a place of healing and teaching. Even though the soul may be in exile, some survivors seem already to have an understanding and experience of a sacred world that sustains them, such experiences are described. To approach the seashore and become involved in the inner world there has to be an insight into the possibility that things might change for the better.

In chapters 5, 6, and 7, three sea voyages narrated by Mark are used, and also the healings that take place immediately after. Chapter 5 focuses on the first sea journey where Jesus, initially asleep in the boat, quells the storm. The account offers insights into how quickly old anxieties can resurface, and feel as if they are swamping the adult. The fear of being overwhelmed and of everything falling apart—of drowning in the power of the past—is explored from the therapeutic and spiritual perspective. In chapter 6, the vision of Jesus walking on the water is seen as an epiphany, where fear is confronted and self-belief begins to be re-established. The disciples' fear of ghosts can be seen to link strongly to the need for survivors of childhood trauma to emotionally confront past powerful figures in the psyche, and their manifestation as internal oppressors. The teaching that takes place on the third sea voyage in chapter 7 is about arriving at an authentic understanding rather than compliance and falsity, and waking up to a new reality. Jesus urges the disciples to open themselves, and being open involves coming to grips with anger and ambivalence, allowing emotions to surface.

Part 3 is about being back on the land again. While appreciating that the night sea journeying is often a spiral rather than linear, the last two chapters, 8 and 9, look at how to integrate the revelations and epiphanies that have taken place. These include balancing the psyche—the crossing and recrossing of the sea that's needed to hold the past experiences in the light of present understanding. One of the insights gained by inner explorations is that while there is no "after" in trauma, for the past cannot be rewritten, new ways of managing and integrating become viable as the soul recovers and spiritual trust deepens. Finally, at the end of the book, there is an appendix with suggested spiritual practices for soul recovery.

# PART 1

# BEFORE ENTERING THE WATER

# 2

# My Soul, Where Are You?

> My soul, my soul, where are you? . . . Do you hear me? I call you . . . are you there? I have returned I am here again . . . Do you still know me? . . . Give me your hand, my almost forgotten soul.[1]

THIS IS THE CRY that Carl Jung made when in deep turmoil following his break with Sigmund Freud, with all the associated loss of status, work, colleagues, and reputation. Embarking on his own night sea journeying, Jung spent many long and lonely hours attending to his derelict and neglected inner world, and then writing down dreams, visions, and fantasies of what he encountered in the deep unconscious. Jung knew that he needed to attend to his damaged soul. In this chapter, what happens to the soul after trauma is explored: the soul may retreat or go into exile; it may also be crowded out by the needs of the psyche to prevent further traumatization through the development of a defensive self-care system.

After trauma, the soul, "the divine spark," earlier defined also as the sense of aliveness and the channel to a full spiritual sense of being, retreats, while the full strength of the psyche's survival system swings into action. The soul may be partly in exile or numb, while the psyche is preoccupied. For the child, and indeed later for

1. Jung, *Red Book*, 232.

the adult, this is like being in an occupied state, preoccupied by what has occurred, even if it can barely be remembered or understood. Soul-numbing means cutting off life-saving relationships to others and reducing the possibility of feeling truly alive in the world. The child's sense of reality, truth, and goodness has been distorted by trauma, and so the capacity of the child for joy and orientation to what is joyous and life-affirming is damaged. The trauma leads to a collapse of trust and faith, leading the child to feel that the world is fundamentally unsafe.

## THE SOUL IN EXILE

For my soul is full of trouble,
and my life draws near to Sheol . . .
I am shut in so that I cannot escape;
my eyes grow dim through sorrow.[2]

The author of Psalm 88 writes of an inner state of despair and desolation that may be familiar to many who have suffered from childhood trauma. The writer voices misery and depression (3–4a); abandonment and rejection (4b–5); self-recrimination and feelings of persecution (6–8); and disconnection from others and from God (5b, 8, 12, 18). Some of the feelings expressed could be interpreted as self-punishment to the extent of suicidal thoughts (10–12). The psalm conveys not only abject misery, but also how the person has had to cut off their self from the complex feelings about what has happened.

Similarly stuck and paralyzed by the past, the soul of the survivor of childhood trauma is locked deep inside, in a way that means any possible movement towards healing is, as the psalm above states, dimmed through sorrow. The soul as the sacred core of our aliveness and an honoring of the spiritual world is shut away, and access prevented by a "protective" self-care system that steps in when life has proved unbearable. In this way the flow of

2. Psalm 88:3, 8b, 9a.

energy is stalled between the unconscious and the ego, between the imperishable world and the transient world, and then access to God and a sense of the divine is often blocked. There is anxious estrangement from the Ground of our Being—what has been called "primal wounding" and a violation to our essential selves.[3]

The term often used is *survival*, and this captures something of the life-and-death feeling. Surviving means that the present life is invariably overshadowed by the threat of the past returning one way or another, while the future offers the potential for further suffering. Trauma means that death and life are no longer so clearly bounded, but rather the space between the two is the place of survival, where many are living what Helen Epstein, amongst others, calls a half-life.[4] This middle part between death and life has been seen as equivalent to Holy Saturday—where Christ descended into hell, on *his* night sea journeying. The place of surviving is between the cross (the trauma) and resurrection (recovery from trauma): between life and death. The theologian Shelly Rambo describes this as the painful middle place, where suffering does not disappear and life does not abound. Trauma survivors exist at an interstice where there is "no clean break from the past, of death behind and life ahead," and where "life persists in the midst of death and death in the midst of life."[5]

Any interest or understanding of something "more than oneself" and of God's all-knowing, all-loving nature is largely irrelevant or denied. Access to transcendent sources of meaning, energy, and value are more or less blocked, and with it the possibilities of self-transformation are deeply affected. The child often holds themselves together, closing off the possibility of further trauma, but also of further spiritual development. They are too fearful of the chaos or disintegration that might follow from a different experience, and anything other to what is already deeply fixed in the psyche. There can be no real openness, no real self-validation, no real joy, and no genuine transcendence.

3. Cf. Firman and Gila, *Primal Wound*.
4. Epstein, *Long Half-Lives*.
5. Rambo, *Spirit and Trauma*, 168, 176.

Joe

I was adopted when I was two years old by really nice, kind people, after being in a fostering set-up where I was neglected, and not given enough food or the right sort of food to eat, or kept clean. When I was tiny, I apparently had something called "failure to thrive," but I can't really remember anything from that time. I've looked it all up of course, and it's when your weight is below that of other children—I was much smaller and shorter than other kids. I was also behind in terms of relating, and so was very quiet and withdrawn, didn't know many words—apparently just sat there on a sofa often in a dirty nappy, a bit floppy, and apparently unresponsive. Later, I thought it must have been my fault that the foster carer didn't bother to look after me, she didn't like me—and that's gone deep. I've not always felt that confident about myself or even liked myself very much.

From when I was adopted until I was a teenager, I think everything was pretty good in the sense that I just got on with it. I remember loving the order of things—every day was predictable. Everything was in its place, and became so familiar—we always had fish pie and apple crumble on a Saturday for lunch, and then chicken and tinned pineapple for pudding on Sunday lunch. My older sister and I would play pretty well together, and we were all keen on sport—it was nice. I love my adoptive parents to bits, and am so grateful they came along when they did, they really put themselves out to help me catch up. I do remember all the effort they put in to help me learn to play and have fun. They've been brilliant, but that sometimes makes me feel bad too—as if I've let them down. I can't shake off the label "failure to thrive."

The other thing is that I don't quite fit, or at least *I think* I don't quite fit. Partly because I'm dual heritage, and mum and dad are both white—my biological father was apparently Indian. My sister is adopted too, and her father was from Trinidad and her mother English like mine—but it didn't seem to bother her the way it did me. Also, mum and dad are both kind and confident of who they are, and kind and *still* confident about me. I'm not

> particularly kind to myself or anyone else—though I am gradually getting better at that, yet even by my early thirties I had no idea of who I was or what the point of my life could possibly be . . . and as for a soul—whatever that is it had certainly failed to thrive as well.
>
> There isn't much to say about my biological mother except she hadn't wanted me, and I didn't know anything about who my father was except that he was Indian. I didn't want to think about them, or what had happened. I didn't want to think about anything, but I found I kept feeling weird, and then even weirder as a teenager—what am I—English or Indian, so where did I fit . . . how was I supposed to be? I switched off, but kept getting into trouble—"underachieving" they called it—I was still failing and not thriving. Then I thought I could become someone else by muscle building and pumping iron . . . but all that pretense couldn't last—eventually I made myself ill, and then I realized I was deeply angry—not the lashing-out sort, just quiet raging, and all I could do was withdraw. I went silent and depressed, and took to my bed. Just lying there—not even looking at anything. Sometimes I slept, and sometimes I just lay and sort of stared at the wall. I felt so tired—worn out, like an old man with no more energy left to make an effort.

Traumatic events, whether single, multiple, or cumulative, are experiences that wound every part of us, and that remain an open wound until what happened can be integrated. When the parent or carer does not, or is unable to, protect their child over a significant part of the child's development from infancy to adolescence, then the child can be overexposed to serious and repetitive stresses and strains. This is trauma that is cumulative and deeply damaging and that leads to lack of trust, low confidence, and discomfort. In some situations, and for different reasons, the mothering person's protective shielding may fail. Sometimes it is because of the excessive impingement by an adult of their own needs and conflicts onto the child; or there is loss and separation from the parent; or when there has been severe physical illness either in the child or adult that creates special demands that are too difficult to meet.

Cumulative trauma becomes life—it's as if one part of the child continues functioning, waking, eating, going to school, but they cannot be truly present or able to live enjoying the moment. This is partly because the child remains wary, waiting for what might happen next. The nervous system becomes tuned by history where even ordinary things may appear a threat; the soul is frozen in anticipation of further damage, and the spirit falters and is subdued.

In his biography of post-traumatic stress disorder, the former Marine and war correspondent Dave Morris describes "small-t trauma" and "big-T trauma," noting that over the course of months or years, small-t traumatic events can add up and become something entirely different. They can become big-T traumas: "Big-T traumas can destroy the soul. . . . The salient factor with these traumas is their ability to make you feel helpless and overwhelmed."[6] Morris is writing about trauma in adulthood, when there can be seen to be a before-trauma and an after-trauma—where the mind works differently after trauma, soul experiences are corroded, and the body too is altered.

However, what happens when the trauma *begins* in early childhood or even infancy, where there can be no conscious sense of *before*-trauma—merely a sense of "*this* is how life *is*?" Trauma is of course always experienced uniquely by individual people, not collectively by dehumanized "victims," and every victim and survivor has a different story to tell. But all traumatic experiences disrupt our well-being, and even if just short term disturbs the individual's psychological growth. How we react to trauma depends on our age, the specific nature of the events and the context it occurs in as well as our inner resilience and psychological needs.

Trauma is what does not go away—it refuses to stay in the past, and is where the past and present conflate: "the two collide to create a perception that the trauma happens now."[7] Rambo writes how trauma persists in symptoms that live on in the body, and fragments of memories that return. She describes this as living in

6. Morris, *Evil Hours*, 52.

7. Arel, *Bearing Witness*, 46.

a place of survival where many are living what has been called a half-life. This is where past trauma distorts time, so that the present is organized with reference to the threat of the past returning one way or another.[8] The inevitable effect of this is to leave the person vulnerable to intense and overwhelming anxieties, which may appear to come from external events and also from internal sources. Why was I not protected from this? How could this happen? Will it happen again? How can I feel better? Can I feel better? Inevitably trust and faith in a benign universe are shattered, and the soul stays in hiding.

The psychoanalyst and pediatrician Donald Winnicott describes how when the child is confronted by fear and pain long before they can manage it, there is a failure in what he calls the "holding environment," where the mothering person is unable to sufficiently care for the infant's needs. This leads to what he described as unthinkable anxiety and possibly a disturbed relationship between the mind and the body that affects our spirit and soul.[9] Often trauma in childhood drives people inwards although on the outside they may appear to have coped. The analyst Joy Schaverien, in her study of boarding school syndrome, describes how some of the boys sent away from home at a young age develop a defensive structure where in order to survive

> a hidden compartment in the self is acquired where such experiences are locked away . . . Emotionally the true self shrinks into a tiny sphere where it is no longer known . . . Deep within is the hidden vulnerable child who trusts no one. The outer presentation is a tough invincible masculine image.[10]

For Evie the trauma began before she could speak and it was only later that she knew what had happened to her.

8. Rambo, *Spirit and Trauma*, 7.

9. Winnicott, *Maturational Processes*, 58.

10. Schaverien, *Boarding School Syndrome*, 187–88.

Evie

> Over the years, I've gathered that after I was born my mother was ill. It was a difficult birth, and for years I felt responsible for causing her this damage, and that's because she regularly said her being ill was my fault. She found looking after me difficult and joyless; it was painful carrying me upstairs to the second floor flat where we lived. Eventually, she was hospitalized for an operation and long convalescence, and so at eighteen months I was fostered; firstly, by my godparents but I turned out to be too difficult for them; and then by a couple whom my father knew from his work. After some months with this family, my mother was recovered enough to have me back, but then kept getting ill and going to hospital. That happened all through my childhood, so I was always worrying that she might be ill again and it would be my fault. I never felt she particularly liked me, and she certainly found showing me love very difficult. She told me that she had wanted a boy, but because she had been so ill my parents had no more children.
>
> I was always frightened of her, she would smack me hard, but I was also terrified of her disappearing again and abandoning me, so I was living the whole time in conflict—not that I knew it, but it was there deep within me—and this unconscious conflict later led to many problems. My dad did his best, but my mother was the one in charge—to my mind all-powerful.

While some amount of lack of care and even torment is inevitable in everyone's childhood, intense or regularly occurring trauma means, as Shengold puts it using psychoanalytic language,

> that the children's subsequent emotional development has been profoundly and predominantly negatively affected; what has happened to them has dominated their motivating unconscious fantasies; and they have become subject to the compulsion to repeat . . . their injurious past.[11]

11. Shengold, *Soul Murder Revisited*, 1.

Emotional abuse is particularly hard to describe as it often includes nothing overt, but is rather an absence of a feeling that the child is enjoyed for their own sake. The child is not celebrated for who they are. The parent's face does not light up when they appear—there is no playful interaction with the parents to enable the soul of the child to authentically come into being. If there is no positive response from those on whom we depend, and over time there is no sense of being valued and valuable, we discover that something dies inside us, and we are not fully alive; we don't know how to play and be spontaneous. This is the decline and eventual retreat of the soul—the true self. Inner resources are needed in order to try to cope with what is happening, and, much later, to cope with what has happened.

Some children are subjected to almost totalitarian control from a powerful parent, or in some terrifying situations by both parents. So-called ordinary family life is replaced by what Judith Herman describes as "capricious enforcement of petty rules, intermittent rewards, and destruction of all competing relationships through isolation, secrecy, and betrayal."[12] Some traumatized children like Joe fear for their own survival, or like Evie worry excessively about the health of their parent. Children who are victims of childhood trauma are usually powerless and feel helpless. In this situation the adult has overwhelmed the less powerful child. The child is trapped and often silenced, there is a binding of the soul, which may become numb or retreat.

The spiritual director and psychotherapist James Finley shares an early memory of abuse from his father:

> I am standing near the window in the living room . . . I am looking at my father coming toward me, I think to pick me up and hold me. Instead, he seizes hold of me and throws me across the room. My face hits the leg of a table. I fall to the ground crying. The place where my face hit the table feels hot. My father walks toward me, stands over me for a moment, then walks away saying

12. Herman, *Trauma and Recovery*, 98–99.

> nothing. This is my first memory. This is how my life as I remember it began. I am three, maybe four years old.[13]

For Finley what began as an initial act of violence became a childhood of cumulative trauma, with long-term implications to do with the deep and strong effects on the soul, mind, and body. Van der Kolk writes:

> Trauma is not just an event that took place sometime in the past; it is also the imprint left by that experience on mind, brain and body . . . It changes not only how we think and what we think about, but also our very capacity to think.[14]

The unexpected and apparently random nature of Finley's father's angry outbursts meant that as a small boy he became hypervigilant. He also became aware that at other times there was a slow build-up.

> I don't know which I dreaded more, the explosive violence that came without warning or those moments when his anger would become more and more intense, letting me know that at any moment I or someone else in the room was going to be hit and that there was nothing any of us could do about it.[15]

Hypervigilance also became a way of life for Evie, who would search her mother's face to find out how she was, and how Evie might please her and be loved. Being good was expected, and smacking was the punishment for disobedience and for doing something wrong. Working out the rules of how to behave, and keeping ahead of what might be asked for, might mean that she was liked. This took up a lot of time.

Many survivors of cumulative childhood trauma recall the unpredictability of family life and random violence and abuse; others remember being subject to a highly organized system of arbitrary rules, often about the smallest thing; some seemed just

13. Finley, *Healing Path*, 4–5.
14. Van der Kolk, *Body Keeps the Score*, 390.
15. Finley, *Healing Path*, 6.

strange, and made no sense—like having the "wrong" expression on the child's face. For some who have experienced cumulative trauma in childhood either in the family or outside, the trauma has been buried deeply, and only partially emerges in adulthood when life events lead to increased vulnerability.

## THE DEFENSIVE SELF-CARE SYSTEM

In childhood, there may be the actual oppressor continuing to traumatize, but alongside this the child may have unconsciously developed a defensive and protective self-care system. This is a way of surviving, and a diversion or way of dissociating from the original trauma, but can also in time become an additional problem. Most children draw on reserves of resilience to find ways to try to manage their fear and upset, so, on the surface, these children may sometimes seem quite alright and unaffected. However, at a deeper level, the child is miserable, and their psyche is developing strategies to survive the psychological aftereffects; this then limits soul energy.

What has happened can get compartmentalized—the focus for the child is on getting through, but this can lead to what has been called affective dissociation, which means that some feelings just go into cold storage, repressed. The child develops ways of emotionally disconnecting, certainly from what is happening or has happened to them. Such a self-care system keeps the child surviving, but in the end leads to further difficulties. Defensive strategies against further trauma can lead to a life dominated by an internal oppressor, possibly even alongside the actual external oppressor. Sometimes the distress also emerges through physical symptoms.

Evie

> When I went to a nursery class, I used to cling to the wall leading to the door of the nursery, scraping my fingers on the stone and crying. I didn't want to leave home and my mother. Unfortunately, the symptoms

got more complicated when I began proper school as I developed a habit of making myself sick every morning. I'd get this tummy ache, which I suppose was tension, and then would try to stop the tummy pain by coughing and coughing and then being sick. We'd moved by then to a new-build estate, and I began school in September. Before then I spent time on a tricycle going round and round the cul de sac, but keeping my eyes firmly on the house. I didn't realize it then, but what I was doing was keeping my eye on the comings and goings of my mother.

What I didn't like about making myself sick, and now looking back it seems so self-destructive, is that I couldn't stop until I reached the bile. Perhaps it was getting deeper and deeper into my anger and distress . . . Somehow it became an accepted way of behaving, my mother would even bring what we called the sick bowl, wait while I retched, and then take it away again tutting and cross. Later I had to wash it out myself. Then I left to go to school. But I also worried before any outing, so even being away from home felt risky.

She was so critical of me and how I looked and behaved, which kept me in a state of anxious despair about ever pleasing her. Sadly, this lack of pleasure and joy has permeated through into my adult life, as has the need to be compliant and try to please others. Decades later I understood my behaviour was called separation anxiety, not school phobia as it was sometimes referred to, because once I was actually at school, I enjoyed it. Through therapy I understood that at a deep unconscious level, I was very anxious about leaving mother in case my repressed rage made her ill, made her leave, or destroyed her. As I've said, her being ill when I was tiny seemed to be my fault, and I went on feeling in some ways responsible for her until she died in old age. The trauma of her early inability to mother me, and her absences through illness became overlaid by this ongoing worry and catastrophic thinking. The symptom of being sick was aimed at me staying with her—though it didn't work, and made her even crosser. Ironically, perhaps that was part of the aim too . . .

The defenses can also take the form of identification with the aggressor,[16] where, as Anna Freud describes it, traumatized children can at times dissociate and become taken over by the behavior of the person who has hurt or abused them. This is not a conscious decision, for the traumatized child's psyche is fragmented, and the mimicking of the abuser can become an automatic response. It is a strange form of protection, as there is a danger of getting stuck with imitating the behavior of the aggressor in attacking oneself, which can become a threat to oneself, or when the behavior is acted out, can be a threat to others.

James Finley gives a good example of this when he writes how he would sometimes hurt himself as a way of feeling relief, and take charge of what felt so out of control:

> When I was taking a shower, I would sometimes hit myself in the face and on my chest and arms and legs as a way to take matters into my own hands by ritualistically reenacting the relief that came as soon as my father hit me or my mother or one of my brothers. I felt ashamed about this secret way of making myself feel better.[17]

If the oppressor or aggressor is the parent, then small children have no alternative other than to be emotionally close to them, but such an enmeshed attachment to an abusive parent can take years to disentangle and lasts long into adulthood, leading to ongoing problems in adult relationships. As both Evie and Joe experienced, infants and babies who are subject to early emotional trauma, abuse, or neglect can find a way of self-holding to take the place of holding by the person who should be looking after and mothering them. However, when the child has been neglected, abused, or critically disappointed, or when random circumstances have led the child to feel that the world is unsafe, then there is a serious collapse in faith and trust in the world, and so the soul, the sense of aliveness, is exiled. This is in part a form of psychic depletion, where the lingering effects of the trauma are found both

16. Freud, "Identification with the Aggressor."

17. Finley, *Healing Path*, 6.

in the body and in some sections of the brain, where our behavior patterns and responses have become distorted. Post-traumatic stress disorder means that the whole nervous system can re-experience aspects of the trauma when something occurs that triggers a memory or a flashback.

The defenses set up by the psyche can strangely be seen as a form of grace by offering protection, but they are also a resistance to healing by becoming a problem in their own right. The lost and orphaned part of the child wants to reach out for love, but the defenses warn against this as they are there to protect the damaged child from re-experiencing what was unbearable pain, which remains present as unprocessed dread. The child is denied the water of life, and the trauma remains unintegrated, lying below the surface. The emotions are unshared and neglected as the feelings about what happened have not been recognized by anyone, and so end up becoming repressed. Yet, sometimes the tension of this may become too great and so, like a dam breaking, the repressed energy is released in a painful crisis and further re-traumatizing. Some children become compliant and good in order to placate the traumatizing adult, constructing an idealized self who lives for others and disregards their own needs. When compliance happens, any spontaneity and joy in being alive becomes derailed, and the child is living under immense strain.

Evie remembered how in primary school, she would sing hymns to her mother while her mother was preparing supper, trying to cheer her up as she complained in the kitchen about all she had to do. It was, she says looking back, particularly poignant to sing: "Jesus, good above all other, gentle child of gentle mother, in a stable born our brother, give us grace to persevere." Without consistent love Evie became increasingly insecure, clinging to a mother who was not able to offer stable kindness. Life goes on as the trauma becomes encoded in the body, until some sort of healing can occur, which is when, as Kalsched states, "the repetitive, addictive, neurotic suffering of Hell gives way to the directed, meaningful, authentic suffering"[18] that ultimately can lead to integration and soul recovery.

The defenses are meaningful and always to be respected, in that they can save a child from breakdown. In that sense they are a blessing, while also being a private hell. Amongst all this confusion the soul retreats. The irony is that many traumatized children go on to distinguish themselves in the external world in terms of achievements and accomplishments, although still suffering in terms of damaged connections with other people and the ability to authentically be in touch with their feelings. It may not be until later in adulthood that the past trauma catches up with the adult—a development that Sigmund Freud famously called "the return of the repressed."[19] The soul of the adult lies dormant like a seed ready to leap into life when that moment comes. First the door into the past has to be opened to find the core of the suffering self, and be drawn to the scent of water and a new life.

18. Kalsched, *Trauma and the Soul*, 89.

19. Freud, "Repression."

# 3

# The Scent of Water

For there is hope for a tree, if it is cut down, that it will sprout again, and that its shoots will not cease.
Though its root grows old in the earth, and its stump dies in the ground, yet at the scent of water it will bud and put forth branches like a young plant.[1]

"'What is the scent of water?'
'Renewal. The goodness of God coming down like dew.'"[2]

THE SOUL NEEDS NOURISHING, but following childhood trauma many are cut off from the living water; they cannot trust the river of life. The traumatized child, and later when they are an adult, often lives on parched land: sometimes overly protected by their defensive self-care system. The place or the people that were trusted turn out not to be safe, and so there is strong disorientation. Some respond by becoming cut off and closed to confident relationality, genuine compassion, joyful pleasure, and authentic intimacy. The river of living water has been largely diverted, or dammed up in some way, or perhaps frozen over so the child walks on ice, unable

1. Job 14: 4–5.
2. Goudge, *Scent of Water*, 285.

to access their soul and true self, and also cut off from any higher wisdom.

Alternatively, some traumatized children, despite finding that there is scarce nourishment for their soul, hold on to some idea of divine presence that then becomes a safe place, and experiences of this are presented in chapter 4. But in this chapter, two ideas are discussed. The first looks at further aspects of the defensive self-care system that can become especially difficult in adulthood: repetition compulsion where the trauma can seemingly endlessly get repeated in various forms, and secondly, the effect of shame on the soul. Both these distressing symptoms can lead the adult to begin to look for a different way of being, and this may be compounded by the gradual breakdown of the defenses, leading to fear and panic. In the second half of the chapter there is an exploration of the deep longing for change and for a cleansing from the past. The experience described early in Mark's Gospel of Jesus' baptism by John is used as a way to explore the desire of change and some form of healing.

## REPETITION COMPULSION

Something has happened to the child. There is an actuality to that event, and yet the victim is, to some extent, left alone with their pain and the imprint on their mind, body, and spirit. There is an unknowability to another's pain that leaves the person suffering alone, and the person is alone again when the trauma resurfaces either in the mind or body, and then the reality of what happened makes it hurt all over again. The experience, so deeply embedded into the psyche, often prevents attempts to deal with it. Paradoxically, despite trying to avoid what feels unbearable there is often a strong, largely unconscious urge to repeat some of what was so damaging, either in a directly recognizable form, or symbolically. This repetition is, at the very least, a sign that something is stuck, and has not been worked through. It remains unintegrated by the psyche.

For James Finley it was a pattern of relating that was recreated, especially in his first marriage. Writing about living in an emotionally disconnected way with what he calls a "dissociative, disconnected survival strategy," he found that he was making decisions that perpetuated the painful and chaotic patterns from childhood. This included marrying the first woman that he had ever dated, and quickly finding that:

> My wife and I seemed gridlocked in argumentative patterns in which my emotionally distancing ways triggered her feelings of emotional abandonment and anger toward me. This, in turn, triggered my childhood fears of being threatened by my father's anger. Round and round we went in patterns of fear, anger, and resentment that we could not understand.[3]

The trauma is repeating itself because it has not yet been properly acknowledged and processed, and so cannot just be a memory. Another tendency of the long-term effects of abuse is for the person who has experienced abuse to adapt to the abuse as a so-called normal part of life: it's just what happened—nothing to see here. This then means being stuck in a way of life where misfortune and mishaps keep recurring and being repeated; this could be called masochism and potentially become addictive, as well as exhausting and demoralizing.

Evie

> As an adult, I kept finding myself being compliant, and agreeing to do all sorts of things I didn't want to do, trying desperately to please other people, usually these older women, by tying myself in knots for their approval, and then having all the physical reactions again. It seemed impossible to stand up for myself, and even if I was asked, I never really knew what it was I wanted to do in situations, until it was too late. Sometimes I didn't see what was going on until I was deeply involved and there seemed no way out. I didn't know my own mind.

3. Finley, *Healing Path*, 99–100.

> I also had to protect myself from bad news about illnesses and separations, and that has had a lasting effect on my relationships. My body can't distinguish what's a real threat, and what might be a threat, and that has just gone on, despite all my attempts—it's so deeply encoded in me. And I'm ashamed of how sometimes I react especially when it's clearly out of all proportion to what's really happening. And I'm ashamed of feeling ashamed . . . ugh! I knew that I had to do something about feeling so rubbish, but didn't know what.

## SHAME AS A SOUL-EATING EMOTION

The long half-life of trauma includes shame. This is essentially a feeling about who we are, and not necessarily about what has happened to us. It was Carl Jung who described shame as a soul-eating emotion, because it affects our relationship with ourselves as well as with others. This is because shame is experienced both through the actual eyes of another person, and the internalized parental eyes that come from our infancy. "You ought to be ashamed of yourself" and "shame on you" can become deeply embedded statements.

Shame is a feeling of loathing and condemnation toward oneself, about the state and nature of one's whole sense of self. Shame motivates the desire to hide, to disappear. We cringe, shrink, wish to disappear at the thought that these facts about ourselves might be observed by another, and thus shame characteristically leads to concealment, to hiding, and to deception. Loss of face, disgrace, and dishonor are close relatives in the family of shame. Shame can also produce a feeling of ineptness, incapacity, and a feeling of not belonging. And so we defend strongly against shame by withdrawal, avoidance (which can take many different forms), attacking others, and attacking the self. Stephanie Arel writes,

> Not addressed, shame is interred, stored in the body to function maladaptively . . . In the process of interment, messages about shame internalized as beliefs, values, and

norms, or externalized through projection onto others, emerge viscerally as affects in the self.[4]

Joe

> At secondary school I began to really, seriously hate my body. It sometimes seemed distorted—too small, too thin, and I thought my head was too big for the rest of me. When I saw myself in mirrors or reflected in shop fronts, I was so ashamed of how I looked. That's why I bulked up my muscles and briefly got into steroids—anything but see myself reflected, and feel so embarrassed. I was going to this gym, it's a sort of fitness center, and one of the guys there said he could get me some of these steroids—I think I was about seventeen then. You shouldn't really take them when you're still growing, but I reckoned I'd stopped growing and been the same height for ages, but despite all the weight lifting and training I was still skinny. You could get all the information you needed at the gym, and I'd look at these guys and think they look great—they've got the secret to looking like a real man, so why not me? And it worked—quite quickly too—I had all these muscles and then for a while people I'd known at school would come up and say "wow, you look great, you used to be skinny but look at the size of you now." I no longer felt ashamed of how I looked, and of myself. I was no longer a weedy little runt.

Joe's trauma happened to him in the first few years of life and during that time it seems that he had never experienced enough love and acceptance for who he was himself. He'd only briefly been loved unconditionally as a tiny baby, and not at all by a neglectful foster parent. He was loved once he was adopted, and Joe knew that, but the early damage remained below the surface, and so hard to repair, and, at a deep level, he felt shame for being unloved. Ideas from developmental neurobiology show that when the infant looks to the mothering figure for approval and instead finds a response indicating disapproval or disgust, the child experiences

4. Arel, *Affect Theory, Shame and Christian Formation*, 46.

shame. If we are exposed to the disapproval of the mothering person then the bond of empathy is breached. The experience is one of falling out of attunement and into a place of affective loneliness; connection is lost, and communication is inhibited, and the more authentic self is felt as an embarrassment. Joe took on this disapproval and disgust and directed it against his own body, and as it turned out against every part of him, including his soul. Eventually this became too much and depression set in.

Over time comes the realization that something will need to change for life to become in any way bearable, let alone enjoyable. The suggestion here is that this hint that things could be different comes from within the psyche, from the soul itself, the life-giver, and is often encouraged by some outside wisdom or influence.

## FEAR AND PANIC

> The light of truth burns without a flicker in the depths of a house that is shaken with storms of passion and of fear. . . . And so I go on trying to walk on the waters of the breakdown.[5]

Over time the defensive self-care system suffers and can become overwhelmed, and when this happens the person will experience fear and perhaps panic attacks, or break down completely. Thomas Merton describes his experiences of this. Surviving the loss of both his parents in childhood, and frequent moves between boarding schools in Britain and with his grandparents in the United States, Merton by any accounts had a difficult and traumatic childhood. His defense seemed to be not to think about any of it, and to keep busy. Writing about the death of his father after a long and protracted illness, Merton as an adult writes:

> What could I make of so much suffering? There was no way for me, or for anyone else in the family, to get anything out of it. It was a raw wound for which there was no

5. Merton, *Search for Solitude*, 22.

> adequate relief. You had to take it, like an animal . . . Try to avoid it, if you could. But you must eventually reach the point where you can't avoid it anymore. Take it. Try to stupefy yourself, if you like, so that it won't hurt so much. But you will always have to take some of it. And it will all devour you in the end.[6]

Merton's childhood losses caught up with him when as a student in New York, and following the deaths of both his grandparents, he had a massive panic attack while traveling on the railway. He was overwhelmed by fear and anxiety: "my head suddenly began to swim . . . as if some center of balance within me had been unexpectedly removed, and as if I were about to plunge into a blind abyss of emptiness without end . . ." Standing up and moving between the rail cars to get some air, Merton found "my knees were shaking . . . so I got back and propped myself against the wall and held on. This strange vertigo came and went . . . I was scared." Finding a doctor in the Pennsylvania Hotel near the station, Merton is told to rest, but fearful of another panic attack, scared about looking out the window, and listening to the blood pounding in his head, he is beset by morbid thoughts:

> And far, far away in my mind was a little, dry, mocking voice that said: "What if you threw yourself out of that window . . ." I thought to myself: "I wonder if I am having a nervous breakdown."[7]

What remained for Merton was fear, and this then extended to worrying about his physical health and whether he might suddenly die. Winnicott calls this annihilation anxiety, linking it back to early experiences in childhood when the child felt terribly unsafe and thought they might not survive.[8] During the first years of being a monk in the Abbey of Gethsemani, especially at times of stress and unacknowledged conflict, Merton experienced more of these same fears and panics, referring to them as the same old

6. Merton, *Seven Storey Mountain*, 82.

7 Merton, *Seven Storey Mountain*, 82, 161–62.

8. Winnicott, "Primary Maternal Preoccupation," 303.

familiar business, and thinking that nobody likes to be afraid. For him the route out lay in spending time in solitude, noting that it is "terror that is driving me into solitude,"[9] and eventually getting permission to spend more time in solitude as a hermit in the woods, "to keep me from folding up completely."[10]

Harry Williams, a priest and theologian, suffered the same symptoms of fear and panic attacks that eventually left him virtually a prisoner in his room, overwhelmed with fear and panic: "I became more and more the victim of terror." His own difficult childhood experiences caught up with him in this dramatic way, eventually leading him into a long psychoanalysis. The Christian insight that stayed with Williams during the worst period of fear and panic "when everything was a black nothing," was the deep mystery that "the cruelly destructive and negative nature of suffering can be seen, if only in a glass very darkly, as charged with positive and creative possibilities."[11]

Some years later Williams was able to write that if you want to find the difference that Jesus made to humankind and go to the New Testament,

> the answer given is the casting out of people's lives fear . . . it is fear which makes men selfish, it is fear which makes them blind, it is fear which makes them mad. Fear casts out love, as love casts out fear. Which of the two therefore am I going to choose?[12]

Williams sees that it is only if we can begin to believe that life is on our side and not against us that we can gain the confidence to begin to turn towards feeling less under attack. This is the confidence that Jesus brings to us. The movement towards this begins with a desire.

9. Merton, *Entering the Silence*, 384
10. Merton, *Search for Solitude*, 27.
11. Williams, *Some Day I'll Find You*, 167, 177.
12. Williams, *True to Experience*, 17.

## THE DESIRE FOR WATER AND CLEANSING

We must surely go the way of the waters, which always tend downward, if we would raise up the treasure . . . and it was a *fish*—"levatus de profundo" (drawn from the deep)—that became the symbol of the saviour, the bringer of healing.[13]

From somewhere deep in the psyche the wish arises for the cleansing power of water: for the past to be washed away; for restitution of well-being and for renewal of health. Perhaps it seems as if the cleansing could make all things new, but the truth is more complex than that. Psychologically the deep water is the unconscious, which lies beneath consciousness, therefore water means spirit that has become unconscious, so the initial whisper of a desire for cleansing and healing comes from the exiled soul. Eventually it will involve bringing previously hidden and repressed experiences into the light and consciousness, and that is the journey across the night sea.

Jung saw water as a living symbol within the psyche, and illustrated this by describing a recurrent dream, dreamt by a theologian who

> stood at the edge of an abyss with a deep valley below, and in it a dark lake. He knew in the dream that something had always prevented him from approaching the lake. This time he resolved to go to the water. As he approached the shore an uncanny darkness fell, and a gust of wind suddenly rushed over the face of the water. Then fear seized him and he awoke.[14]

In the dream the theologian begins to descend into his own depths, and the way leads him to the mysterious water, over which the wind blows. There then occurs the miracle that is a gust of wind rushing over the surface. The theologian associates this to the Gospel account of the pool of Bethesda in John 5:2, where an

13. Jung, *Archetypes*, paras. 37–38.

14. Jung, *Integration of the Personality*, 66.

angel descends and touches the water, which thus receives healing power, so that the sick can be healed by entering the water when it is swirling. In the dream Jung cites, it is this spirit that blows across the water. This is an unseen presence with its own power to stir things up, to make changes, and perhaps to heal, which then threatens the dreamer's sense of control, and of what he himself makes of his life. When the spirit appears spontaneously it is like an apparition, and fear takes over the dreamer's mind. Thus, the dream of the theologian is quite right in showing him that at the water, he will be able to reattain the consciousness of the living spirit. However, there is strong resistance from the dreamer's ego, which holds that the spirit is only something that comes from above, a soaring over the dubious and worthless things that come from below—so the theologian wakes up from the dream.[15] He awoke as the fear took over from the desire to understand the psyche, and begin the process of soul recovery.

The process of ceremonial washing and cleansing is found in the religious and symbolical rite of baptism. In its original form it was a washing clean and a purification ritual, with immersion almost unto the point of death, so it included great fear, and then a rising back into the world, which could be experienced as a rebirth. In Mark's Gospel, and before the calling of the disciples and the ministry of healing and teaching, Jesus is baptized by John the Baptist, who is calling people to repentance, and to confess what they have done, and indeed, what may have been done to them: to own up to their darkness and the shadows of the past.

> In those days Jesus came from Nazareth of Galilee and was baptized by John in the Jordan. And just as he was coming out of the water, he saw the heavens torn apart and the Spirit descending like a dove on him. And a voice came from heaven, "You are my Son, the Beloved; with you I am well pleased."[16]

15. Jung, *Integration of the Personality*, 66.

16. Mark 1:9–11.

How can this baptism be significant to those who were traumatized in childhood? Significantly, Jesus comes to John willing to be judged, but as the theologian John Dunne reminds us, what happens at this point is that Jesus "who is ready to take his place among sinners, receives and experiences unconditional acceptance from God . . . He came to receive condemnation for his past and received instead unconditional acceptance."[17]

Most traumatized children feel responsible for what has happened to them. Joe felt he was unlovable, and so he was ill-treated; Evie felt her birth had led to ongoing physical illness for her mother, and so she, Evie, had to take on the responsibility for keeping her mother alive. Here, in the baptism of Christ, is an immediate breakthrough into God's unconditional love. Every child is "the beloved"; with each child God is "well pleased." The cleansing that the water brings is the promise of a mysterious mercy, pouring down in great abundance. Thomas Merton understood this grace, so that he could write in God's voice:

> What was vile has become precious. What is now precious was never vile. I have always known the vile as precious: for what is vile I know not at all.
>
> What is cruel has become merciful. What is now merciful was never cruel. I have always overshadowed Jonas with My mercy, and cruelty I know not at all. Have you had sight of Me, Jonas, My child? Mercy within mercy within mercy . . .
>
> What was fragile has become powerful. I loved what was most frail. I looked upon what was nothing. I touched what was without substance, and within what was not, I am.[18]

The baptism of Christ shows the traumatized our great destiny, that we too can be out in the world, loved, and graced by divine presence. Mark's account is full of symbolism: emergence from the water, the opening of the heavens; the spirit in the form of a dove; the voice of God, and Jesus alone seeing the vision, and

17. Dunne, *Search for God in Time and Memory*, 9.

18. Merton, *Sign of Jonas*, 354.

standing at the center of the symbols that speak about him. Here there is the uniting of the above with the below, the conscious with the unconscious, the water below and the spirit above. The account from so long ago is also mediating a timeless reality of the existence of each one of us. It is a challenge to the status quo: the defensive self-care system with all its repetition compulsions and defenses; and it is a confrontation with shame and the shame of feeling ashamed, and overwhelming fear and panic. There is a sense of new beginnings, and an identity that has been obscured by the past trauma. As Diarmuid McGann writes:

> It is trying to pass on to me something about my life. It strives to give me knowledge that I should have but don't have. It speaks the essential. The symbols cluster together to speak to me; they are connecting me with the great archetypes of my religious history. Wind, water, a voice, speak, and they speak of the sacred. By entering them I enter the sacred. By listening to them, I hear the sacred, and I allow it to speak to me.[19]

As the desire for cleansing water begins to seep into awareness, so the adult who was traumatized as a child needs to find a way to listen.

> Evie
>
> Things reached a head when my mother told me that she was feeling very low and finding it hard to eat. I was visiting with the children who were about three and six at the time, so I was in my late twenties, had a professional job, and appeared to be functioning pretty well, but I immediately became a small child when I heard this. The old stomach ache reappeared, and I worried and fretted. There seemed to be only one thing, which was to leave my present life, and go back and live with my parents again to try to make everything better. It felt like I was caught right back in the past. It was only when trying to explain this to my husband who was incredulous at my suggestion, that I seemed to come out of this

19. McGann, *Journeying Self*, 16.

> state of mind. What was I thinking? I was thinking as I had done as a small child, and it hadn't worked then. At that point I knew I needed to sort myself out. I needed to try to understand what was going on, and cleanse myself from what was beginning to feel like very toxic and damaging thinking.

The symbolism of cleansing by water is an introduction to a long process: Thomas Merton calls it "a continuous dynamic of inner renewal." An actual baptism happens only once and can mean something and nothing, but a spiritual baptism is something different. This is the desire to be washed and renewed in God; in other words, a spiritual awakening to take a new direction and make a change to the old way of being. This can happen many times in someone's life. It is "A continuous rebirth, in which the exterior and superficial life of the ego-self is discarded like an old snake-skin and the mysterious, invisible self of the Spirit becomes more present and more active."[20]

## THE GRADUAL MOVEMENT TO BECOME MORE OURSELF

Carl Jung had inscribed over the entrance to his house in Zurich: "Vocatus atque non vocatus, Deus aderit," which translated from the Latin is, "Whether summoned or not, God will be present." Jung believed that all of us, to some extent, are on a spiritual path of what he called individuation. This is usually unconsciously, when "it means no more than that the acorn becomes an oak, the calf a cow, and the child an adult."[21] However, if we can choose to take this path consciously, then Jung saw that as the true spiritual achievement.

So, what does individuation mean? The analyst June Singer was asked at an oral examination on individuation how she might explain the process briefly to someone who knew nothing about it.

20. Merton, *Love and Living*, 199.

21. Jung, *Answer to Job*, para. 755.

Having prepared for the oral with lots of academic resources, she was very taken aback, before an image entered her unconscious.

> It is as though you were sitting in a little sailing boat in the middle of the Zurichsee [Lake Zurich], and had no idea how to manage a sailboat. If the current was right and the wind was right, you might get to where you were going sooner or later. Or you might bob around indefinitely and get nowhere. Or a storm could come up and you could be overturned and the whole project end in disaster. But begin the Process, guided by another who has been through it . . . and it is all different. . . . You learn how to take into account the structure of the boat itself, how it is made and how it responds to the water and the wind. The boat is comparable to your own personality. You learn about the currents in the lake, these correspond to the realities of life in which you are situated and which are somewhat unpredictable. You learn about the winds, which are invisible and less predictable, and these correspond to those spiritual forces which seem to give direction to life without ever showing themselves. In learning to sail you do not change the current of the water nor do you have any effect on the wind, but you learn to hoist your sail and turn it this way and that to utilize the greater forces which surround you. By understanding them you become one with them, and in doing so are able to find your own direction—so long as it is in harmony with, and does not try to oppose, the greater forces in being. You may still have to face dangers—there may be swift currents or wild winds at times, but somehow you do not feel helpless any longer.[22]

Individuation means becoming an "in-dividual," and, so implies both our own uniqueness and becoming one's own self: becoming less divided within ourselves through the past and present conflicts; becoming more and more of our own full self, and having less of it projected, or repressed, or split off, and denied. Thus, it can be linked to the promise from Jesus Christ of having "life

22. Singer, *Boundaries of the Soul*, 9–10.

and having it abundantly."[23] Jung understood our spiritual needs to be as real as hunger and the fear of death, as basic, as profound, as essential. He came increasingly to think that the healthiest spiritual aim, that is, the one of most benefit to the individual, is to try to become more and more fully and truly who we essentially are. This is what starts to happen on night sea journeying.

23. John 10:10.

# PART 2

# NIGHT SEA JOURNEY

# 4

# Approaching the Seashore

"Ho, everyone who thirsts, come to the waters."[1]

On the seashore of endless worlds children meet.
Tempest roams in the pathless sky, ships are wrecked in the trackless water, death is abroad and children play.
On the seashore of endless worlds is the great meeting of children.[2]

## THE SYMBOLISM OF THE SEASHORE

The myth of the night sea journey starts by setting off from a place of exile, with eyes on the horizon for the promised land. But you have to get to the water's edge first. The seashore is a liminal place: behind the firm land, but ahead the deep sea; behind the familiar and in front the unknown. Here is the place of opposites and of transition, and, as the journey toward soul recovery begins, so the place of setting off assumes great importance. Here life is on the edge of something new, here is the moving water, with its rising and

1. Isaiah 55:1.
2. Tagore, "On the Seashore."

falling waves, a great contrast to the dried, stuck, occupied place. The seashore is a place of mystery, as Rachel Carson describes.

> Who has known the ocean? Neither you nor I, with our earth-bound senses, know the foam and surge of the tide that beats over the crab hiding under the seaweed of his tide pool home; or the lilt of the long, slow swells of mid-ocean, where shoals of wandering fish prey and are preyed upon, and the dolphin breaks the waves to breathe the upper atmosphere . . . To sense this world of waters known to the creatures of the sea we must shed our human perceptions of length and breadth and time and place, and enter vicariously into a universe of all-pervading water. For to the sea's children nothing is so important as the fluidity of their world.[3]

By the sea important lessons are to be learned, and change can happen. Along the seashore, Jesus teaches the multitudes and heals those who come to him from every direction. While he is also teaching in synagogues, Jesus' teaching beside the sea moves beyond traditional limits, opening out into something infinite and away from the usual constraints and beyond traditional limits.

What is the symbolic significance of the sea water? Water has been seen as the cradle of all things to which all things must return, and as the origin of life. The philosopher Heraclitus, about 500 years before Christ, spoke of the transition between all the elements where everything flows, and where the cosmos itself is engaged in a permanent circular movement: earth becomes water, water becomes earth, and in this permanent transition and change, everything is in fact one. In the sea nothing stands still, and everything is perpetually being remade in a constant state of becoming. And under a reflecting surface there are unsuspected hidden depths. It is a place of secrecy.

Dealing with what has been kept repressed and shut down in the unconscious is the journey toward soul recovery for those who have experienced trauma in childhood. Dealing with what has happened is a matter of spiritual being or nonbeing. All those

3. Carson, "Undersea," 63.

who have met with the experience suggested in the theologian's dream know that the treasure lies in the depths of the water, a treasure that calls out to be salvaged. As in the parable of the hidden treasure in the field, in Matthew 13:44, the treasure has to be dug up from the depths of the earth, it has to be to be uncovered to be recovered. In the same way, the pearl of great price, in Matthew 13:45–46, comes from the ocean bed. The pearl, interestingly, is made by molluscs as a protection against irritants that sneak into their soft tissue. The pearl of great price is born of suffering, and is created as a response to pain. It has to be discovered not just in the ocean bed, but from the very insides of the oyster.

## THE SEASHORE AS A PLACE FOR SPIRITUAL OPENINGS

In the Gospel accounts the seashore is presented as a place of healing, discipleship, and teaching. In Mark's Gospel, he calls the large, inland, fresh water lake the Sea of Galilee, and both alongside it and on its surface a number of important events take place in the course of Jesus' ministry. On the seashore Jesus calls his first disciples, and immediately they leave the sea and follow him.

> As Jesus passed along the Sea of Galilee, he saw Simon and his brother Andrew casting a net into the lake—for they were fishermen. And Jesus said to them, "Follow me and I will make you fish for people." As he went a little farther, he saw James son of Zebedee and his brother John, who were in their boat mending the nets. Immediately he called them; and they left their father Zebedee in the boat with the hired men, and followed him.[4]

The seashore here acts as a setting for radical change, the place on the edge where life can take you in a new direction, and away from the usual way of functioning. Allowing our imagination to freely associate with what we read or hear in these Gospel stories, one way of reflecting on this account is the idea that the

4. Mark 1:16–20.

person living with the aftereffects of trauma tends to spend much of their time preoccupied with what has happened, even if this occurs below conscious awareness. The fishermen in the Gospel are invited to lay down their long-established routine of fishing and caring for their nets—picking the nets apart, and mending them when they become torn over and over again.

What's the invitation? It is a call away from the usual way of doing things into something other. It is an invitation to become truly alive. Using this as a metaphor: The part of the person that longs for healing searches for a way to lay the trapping nets of their defensive self-care system down, and to stop rushing to repair any untoward opening up of the defenses. There is the desire to find a new path and way of living life more fully. Jesus calls the disciples to a new orientation: away from the past self-preoccupations and habits, and instead to be in relationship with others. The path out of the trauma is to search for others to connect with (as in the metaphor of the disciples fishing for people). It is to move to become involved again in the world, but in the company of Jesus, who will help this happen. Allowing for this is accepting the necessity for change, and for losing control over how things currently are in the stuck state.

The invitation for the disciples is to move away from catching and killing cold-blooded fish and instead to connect with a different "fish": the passionate Christ, symbolized in the use of the Greek word "ichthys" or "ichthus," which means fish (where it is used as an acronym for Jesus Christ, God's Son, Savior). The invitation for survivors of a traumatized childhood is to walk bravely into the waters of life.

Evie recounts how as a young adult on holiday near the sea, she walked alone late one evening towards the seashore. This is from the diary entry she wrote at the time:

Evie

It's a misty night, grey sea mists so far that the sky is grey, the sea and the sand are grey, the cliffs are shrouded in grey—I feel an urgency to move deeper towards the sea—into deeper magic levels. Such a spiritual atmosphere already—a place and time not for earth bound humans. I walk towards the sea, like in a trance, I feel possessed by the strange atmosphere and the sound of the waves breaking on the shore. Out of the blue an odd thought comes to mind—let me see God—and within minutes I become overwhelmed by my strangeness. It is as if I am no longer me. I have become part of the grey, nothing separate. I see something swirling, jumping or turning in the water—is it a fish or a piece of rubbish. I want to look and walk into the water. The water is warm to my feet and almost translucent—irresistible but strange. Then I feel great fear and don't want to look in the water in case something bad is there.

I fight to control myself—trying to break what feels like a spell. It is the oddest feeling. My first thought about this unknown feeling is that it is a taste of hell, of madness, but when I was in the strangeness I felt at peace. As I climb back to the top of the cliff and the bright lights and noise of the bar, two birds wheel overhead. Behind me the mists enfold the beach—holding a secret time and space. Something stirs within me. I walk back on the grass.

Looking back, this happened when I didn't understand why I was so trapped in the past way of behaving and reacting to events. I didn't really know I was trapped either, but I was, I see now, very restricted in who I was being, or pretending to be. I needed something outside me to break in—but what and how? I turned to God: but who or what did that mean—I hadn't a clue.

## SPIRITUAL AWARENESS THAT GOD IS PRESENT WITH US IN SUFFERING

Some survivors of childhood trauma, despite everything, seem already to have an understanding and experience of a sacred world that sustains them, even though their soul is in a state of desolation or exile. Where this is the case a form of spiritual awareness can sometimes be a way of coping with what has happened. Perhaps this may seem defensive, but it can also provide great solace and strength for the child. The defensive self-care system, discussed in chapter 2, while causing difficulties as in the accounts from Evie and Joe, can also act, as explained in chapter 3, in one way as a form of grace, of a belief that God is present alongside the suffering.

It can also be the case that frightening trauma can somehow break the child open to another dimension of reality. In that situation the spiritual world, and for some a sense of Presence—of not being alone—can offer great comfort and consolation, and can also alleviate fear. It may be that the child who is traumatized is often forced into another reality, and so becomes a citizen of two realms: the actual painful reality, and, a spiritual world and an imaginative space in the head to help the child survive this. James Finley writes how his mother would tell the children to pray for strength from God to cope with the frightening things that happened when her husband, their father, was angry.

> One night, when I was about four years old, I remember lying in bed in the dark, feeling very sad and afraid because I could hear my father yelling at my mother outside the door. I knew that at any moment he might hit her. I was feeling sad and afraid because earlier that day he had yelled at me and maybe had hit me. I felt sad and afraid because I knew that the next day, if he wanted to, he would hit me again and there was nothing that anyone could do to stop him.
>
> Lying there in the dark, listening to my father raging at my mother, I took what my mother had taught me to heart. I prayed the way frightened children pray, asking God to help me endure the ongoing terror and sadness

> that permeated my life in those days. In a moment I cannot remember, God heard my prayer, came to me in the dark, and took me to a secret place in God where the violence couldn't find me.[5]

Finley describes how after that, when the violence began Finley's father didn't know that he was only hitting the other little boy—what Finley calls "that effigy of myself that others could see. He did not know the more real me, who was safely hidden away in the secret place in God that my father knew nothing about." While later as an adult he recognized that this was a dissociative state where he withdrew from reality, as a child his experience was that God came to him, and merged with him so that he was not alone in the dark. Over the next few years Finley found much consolation in church and especially in the Mass: "I was initiated into the mysterious ways in which the polar opposite realms of trauma and transcendence meet and merge to form a bittersweet alchemy."[6]

In their dreams, these same polar opposites of trauma and transcendence are found for some of those who experience trauma in childhood. Sometimes as they sleep there are glimpses of a different way of being grounded in immaterial realities that remain largely inaccessible to people who live mostly in one world. For some children there can be a different reality experienced with a loved toy or companion animal who can absorb and compensate for the other traumatic reality.

Rebecca Parker's childhood trauma took place when she was four and violently orally raped by a man who lived in the neighborhood and who "befriended" and groomed small children before abusing them. When the little girl was attacked there was a moment when she was close to being killed. In that experience of extreme fear and violence Parker felt what she calls "a Presence" that could hold her fear, and somehow sustain her. She felt that this Presence was stronger than the rapist and could encompass her terror. The Presence was also full of compassion and was deeply

5. Finley, *Healing Path*, 7.

6. Finley, *Healing Path*, 7–8.

connected with her and also with the abuser, and she sensed that if she died the Presence would still be with her.

> The man did stop short of killing me, and I think it was because some part of him could not ultimately deny the knowledge that he was raping God. Not that I was God, obviously, but that the Presence was there . . . I know that had he killed me, it would have been because he completely denied the Presence. Such denial is entirely possible and happens all the time.[7]

Years later, when a theologian and writer, Parker had to open herself to the deepest knowing and remembering of what had happened to her. She left the shore and entered the deep waters, and below the surface encountered the feelings of terror and sorrow that she had kept at bay; and then acknowledged why and how she had constructed after the abuse a good and self-sacrificing self that ignored her own distress. Parker suffered from a near-death experience in the horrendous abuse that happened to her, and while for her there was also a moment of revelation, she is clear that in no way can abuse and trauma ever be seen as a blessing, and certainly no one needs to suffer for God to be revealed to us. For her, faced with this life-threatening violence, a sense of life-giving grace was also present. For some traumatized children a positive connection to numinous experiences beyond the immediate abusive environment can have a healing effect, because it brings within "something more than," and a sense of the mystical and mysterious.

Donald Kalsched, the Jungian analyst, describes his work with Jennifer, who had experienced serious trauma as a little girl, and who came into therapy saying that she had lost her soul. There were fleeting moments when she felt that her soul had returned to her—such as when painting alone in her studio, or sometimes when alone in nature, but most of the time she felt devoid of value and self-worth. Convinced of her own lack and badness, she suffered terribly, but mostly based on self-attacks and self-criticism.

7. Brock and Parker, *Proverbs of Ashes*, 211–12.

> It was as though, in the space inside which her soul had vacated a dark mocking spirit had moved in, a mental spirit that negated everything and filled her with despair and hopelessness. . . . She was surviving, but she was not living.[8]

As the therapy progressed, the woman was able to draw on a memory that helped her towards self-compassion—a transcendent experience which she called a visitation from a presence of light: a presence that she interpreted as an angel, and a power that had supported her to live. At the time of the angel visiting, Jennifer was seven years old, and near death, having been terribly injured through abuse by a relative. Inspired by another little girl patient in the next hospital bed who was coloring a picture, Jennifer thought there might be reason to live. However, her recovery was slow, and at times doubtful, with recurring debilitating episodes of peritonitis. She had been given a box of watercolors, but despite looking longingly at the colors she couldn't see what use it could be.

> The angel when it came to her, was in the midst of soft white-yellow light beside her to the right. Neither male nor female, it was at once terrible and cool and somehow unsurprisingly familiar. Calmly and caringly, the ethereal messenger declared without preamble. "You don't have to continue; it's all right to let go now." The presence paused then continued, "if you decide to stay it won't be easy."[9]

Jennifer remembered how it was tempting to let go and not call out for help with her pain, but then her eyes fell on her box of watercolors and in particular a color called Rose Madder—she thought I need to use this color—how can I leave earth without using it. I need to paint, so she told the angel she had to stay. With the angel's visit came a quiet sense of belonging, a knowing that she was a part of something greater than herself. Her pain had been witnessed. She called for help and gradually got physically better. As an adult she became a painter. Working on the memory of the

8. Kalsched, *Trauma and Soul*, 32.

9. Kalsched, *Trauma and Soul*, 33.

angel gradually began to help her reanimate her soul, and begin to integrate it into her body.[10]

Remaining in fear and confusion, and repeating, or becoming entangled in acting out the trauma either inside ourselves or with another, means that our soul remains estranged from God. This is the occupied state discussed in the previous chapter, where one is exiled from God's self-giving act, caught up solely in the past. But can God be found in the site of the trauma—not as a way of managing or disassociating from it, but rather as the very channel for healing and soul recovery?

One way of thinking about this is to have faith that Jesus visits the place of trauma, where the woundedness is seen and also accepted. The wounded and traumatized Christ's radical, unconditional acceptance of all of us is the healing that comes from beyond us. Through the wounds of Christ, our own wounds can also be healed. The soul recovery is to move to the place of feeling that we are loved and loveable, that we are part of God's story and sustained by God whether we know it or not. The night sea journeying is a descent into awakening the healing of the depth dimension. It involves suffering, yet also experiencing Christ's energy and engaging with his love in the hurting places. Regrounding in the spiritual dimension can work alongside any therapeutic work. The stirring of sustaining love in our depths and connectedness with God deepens our capacity to be open, and to be more sensitive to our hurting places and eventually to others.

## MOVING INTO THE WATER

To walk metaphorically into the waves lapping on the shore there has to be an insight into the possibility that things might be different, that perhaps something could change, and that something *has* to change. Perhaps it is the feeling that one cannot continue in the half-life of trauma, with a landscape pitted by pain, fear, shame, outrage, and humiliation. Perhaps there has been a small

10. Kalsched, *Trauma and the Soul*, 31–33.

insight into life beyond the past—from something that is read, or from something that has been watched in a film or a documentary, from some music that moves us, or something someone has said that affects and guides us. In all sorts of ways, the soul can nudge us towards healing. For Joe it was a series of dreams—or rather nightmares, and then a postcard.

Joe

> I was having terrible trouble sleeping, feeling a bit crazy and not sure what to really do with my life, and all mixed up about who I was and especially about how I looked . . . but when I did sleep, I had these frightening dreams. It usually involved being chased by big angry men—sometimes they were black guys and sometimes white . . . In the dreams I was always tiny—really skinny and small like I used to be as a kid. Well, I am still a bit small . . . but these men were huge. In the nightmare, I could get to my mum and dad's house and shut the door, but then I could hear the men round the back, or if I rushed to the back door they began coming in through the windows, or even once down a chimney—though that wouldn't have been possible in real life. Then the dreams got even worse as it wasn't huge men chasing me, but huge animals trying to bite me, and I would wake as I felt their teeth on my arm or leg. It got so that I didn't want to sleep then, and I found I was feeling angry and exhausted all the time.
>
> I was all over the place, one minute happy and then one minute sad or angry. I was pretty irritable with everyone, but couldn't see what to do about it. Part of me wanted to hurt the people around me, and then I thought perhaps it's me I want to hurt . . . But then I had this dream where I was actually hurting myself . . . banging my head on the floor, and against the wall. I felt pretty sick of everything . . . I was barely hanging on, but I know now I was searching—but with no idea what for. I guess I was longing for someone to help me, but if they tried, I was furious. For one summer I spent most of the time in bed, half dozing trying to catch up on my sleep,

or watching TV. I didn't want to go out or do anything. Then I got a postcard from my sister. It was of a beautiful beach in Thailand. She'd gone with a group of friends, and the picture was of sand and the sea, and palm trees, and a blue sky. On the card she wrote:

Hey Joe Bro [that's what she called me]. Why not get out of bed? There's a whole world to see out here and it's amazing. We've one chance at this life so don't waste it, open the door, come on out and try it! Love you.

I remember I looked at the card for a long, long time imagining her there, and loving her for having a good time. Then I got out of bed and went and phoned for an appointment with the GP. When I saw her, the doctor suggested anti-depressants . . . but the first lot didn't seem to work, although it took months to find that out, and then I felt I'd failed my mum, dad, and sister all over again by being such a miserable git after all they'd done for me. But the next lot of pills started to shift something in my mood, and I began to go out.

I knew something more had to happen but I didn't know what, and I was beginning to feel desperate. I felt I was only half alive. I went out one night with my friend Mike. We'd gone to school together and I liked him, he'd stood up for me a couple of times when I was being bullied so we used to hang about together—but he'd been in a mess too—taking various drugs and pretty dependent on weed to get him through every day, and he told me about his hang-ups and how he'd gone to get help, and found the 12-step programme through Narcotics Anonymous. I dismissed it all at the time, as I wasn't into drugs or drink for that matter, but the conversation stayed with me and started me thinking.

In the previous chapter we visited the work of the theologian Shelly Rambo on living with the aftereffects of trauma where life and death are no longer so clearly separated. The lives of Evie and Joe both continued after trauma, but without the relief of recovery. They remained stuck in the half-life of this middle time. In Christian creeds, Jesus Christ is said after the crucifixion to have descended to hell, where he searched for lost souls: "he went and made a proclamation to the spirits in prison."[11] On this endless day in between, Christ went to the dark abyss of deep suffering, and reaching down pulled the captives from their stuck, imprisoned states of mind, breaking down the doors locked on the inside, and freeing all who were bound. This release of those in the space between trauma and recovery awaits on the far side of the night sea journey, emerging out there from the depths: "Out of the depths I cry to you, O Lord . . . My soul waits for the Lord more than those who watch for the morning."[12] In the theologian Belden Lane's reflections on Holy Saturday he includes this:

> Disclosing a God who's present in the worst things that can happen. This is a God who not only descends into the hell of my loss, but allures me into a new reality, revealing who (and whose) I am.
>
> The outrageous truth of Holy Saturday is that those held hostage in the gulag of the damned are set free and loved beyond measure . . . by a God who summons them to an audacious affair of the heart. "Don't be afraid," Christ says. "I am the First and the Last . . . the Living One; I was dead and I'm now alive. The keys to death and Hell are mine."[13]

There *can* be movement in the stuck middle place, in the occupied inner territory: a movement where something living emerges unexpectedly out of what appears to be empty or even dead. The shift contains the past, but also looks to the future. The small movement is laden with suffering, but moving towards the possibility of something new with less torment, described by Rambo as "weary love making its way through the chaos of hell."[14] It is at this point that the hidden and damaged soul cautiously turns toward the light even amidst the apparent impossibility of anything really changing. McGann writes:

11. 1 Peter 3:19.
12. Psalm 130:1, 5.
13. Revelation 1:17–18, in the quote from Lane, "Christ's Descent," 152.
14. Rambo, *Spirit and Trauma*, 56.

> I come to the water well insulated against anything really happening. Nevertheless I come hoping against hope, with some expectation that . . . water will help to change my life . . .
>
> The sand is message, the sand is call, the sand is invitation.
>
> "I must go down to the seas again, to the lonely sea and the sky," said the poet John Masefield, and so I arise to go from the sand to the water.[15]

As we enter the water, in our imagination we feel first of all its coolness, and its distinctive difference from the sand. The water surrounds us, as we walk carefully keeping our balance and checking out any pitfalls. Then comes the realization that our past is not left on the beach.

> Some of it is still with me in my fears, cares, history. How can I get beyond the history? Is the water beloved lover, or cruel judge, the merciful upholder or the destroying power? Will she nourish or swallow? Somehow I know that I am called to enter her irrespective and let go. . . . Somewhere beyond my fear, beyond my control, beyond both my desire and terror, I know I am afloat. Something in me is held by something even greater.[16]

And a voice that makes no sound tells the survivor that "you are my beloved child; on you my favour rests." The spiritual baptism into the water of life begins.

15. McGann, *Journeying Self*, 17.

16. McGann, *Journeying Self*, 17.

# 5

# Storm at Sea

Save me, O God,
for the waters have risen to my neck.
I have sunk into the mud of the deep
and there is no foothold.
I have entered the waters of the deep
and the waves overwhelm me.

Do not let the deep engulf me
nor death close its mouth on me.[1]

EVERY PERSON WHO WAS traumatized as a child seeks a cessation of the suffering that lingers from the past and that is casting its long shadow over the present. There is a yearning for healing and for restoration. There is a longing to become a whole person, where history can become history, and remain as history. Childhood trauma can leave us in a state of being exiled from God's self-giving love, and instead living in fear and confusion. We are estranged, continually acting out the trauma from the past—either consciously or unconsciously. Our soul, our true self, longs for things to be different, and it is from this, the deepest part of ourselves that the motivation to change begins to occur. In this

1. Psalm 69:1–2, 15, as rendered in Johnson, ed., *Benedictine Daily Prayer*.

chapter, Jesus' calming of the storm is discussed, and the healing that happens afterwards on the other side of the sea crossing.

However, despite positive intentions as the familiar land is left behind and the night sea journeying begins, old anxieties tend to resurface, and associated defences quickly try to protect the person from further trauma. For others who set out on this inner journeying, the defenses feel as if they are being overwhelmed, and there is a fear of everything falling apart—a fear of breakdown and drowning in the powers of the past. This fear of being overwhelmed is explored from a psycho-spiritual perspective.

## DARKNESS AND THE BEATING WAVES

Consider Mark's description of the first sea voyage taken by Jesus with the disciples.

> On that day, when evening had come, he said to them, "Let us go across to the other side." And leaving the crowd behind, they took him with them in the boat, just as he was. Other boats were with him. A great gale arose, and the waves beat into the boat, so that the boat was already being swamped. But he was in the stern, asleep on the cushion; and they woke him up and said to him, "Teacher, do you not care that we are perishing?" He woke up and rebuked the wind, and said to the sea, "Peace! Be still!" Then the wind ceased, and there was a dead calm. He said to them, "Why are you afraid? Have you still no faith?" And they were filled with great awe and said to one another. "Who then is this, that even the wind and the sea obey him?"[2]

This boat journey begins for Jesus in the evening—a time of fading daylight and darkness descending, but also a time of quietness after the day, and a time for something different to emerge. Sometimes darkness is not frightening, it can offer the possibility of revelation, for darkness can be a time for creativity and intimacy,

2. Mark 4:35–41.

and there is always the white light of the moon. Erich Neumann, philosopher and student of Jung, states:

> It is . . . in the cool reflected light of the moon, when the darkness of consciousness is at the full, that the creative process fulfils itself; the night, not the day, is the time of procreation. It wants darkness and quiet . . . The moon is Lord of life in opposition to the lethal devouring sun. The moist nighttime is the time of sleep, but also of healing and recovery.[3]

The Jungian Anne Baring reminds us that the moon controls the tides, and that the essential myth of the moon is one of transformation.

> It is the light shining in darkness, the light that is always changing, yet always the same. The moon is the symbol of the secret, instinctual workings of things that take place "in the dark" beneath the outward appearance of life, beneath the surface of consciousness.[4]

However, in Mark's account, while there indeed may come revelation, the boat journey is far from easy—with squally winds, lowering clouds, and a storm at sea, and there is no mention of moonlight. The unexpectedness of this change of weather points to the difficulty of the crossing, with fear, risk, and uncertainty to the fore. Wind and water are of course important symbols in the Bible, and when combined together herald significant events: such as in the creation story where a wind from God sweeps over the water (Genesis 1:2); and in the crossing of the Red Sea (Exodus 14: 21), where Moses stretches out his hand, and God sweeps the sea with a strong east wind and the waters are divided. In both these accounts the activity of wind and water is followed by a change, and movement out of chaos into union. Biblical theologian Ched Myers explains, "The wind and sea as obstacles derive from the ancient Semitic mythic personification of cosmic forces of chaos

3. Neumann, "On the Moon," 91.

4. Baring, *Dream of the Cosmos*, 68.

and destruction."[5] While Elizabeth Malbon, writing about Mark's Gospel, understands that: "This destructive, chaotic power of the sea is the very power Jesus confronts and overcomes in ordering the sea by stilling the storm . . ."[6]

From a psychological perspective, the crossing over to the other side of the Sea of Galilee in Mark's Gospel can also be seen symbolically as bringing two parts of the self together. The difficulty of this is portrayed by the violence of the storm that terrifies the disciples in the boat, who see the power of the waves as an advent of annihilation and death. The disciples are unaware of the purpose of their journey, and "they betray their profound fear of abandonment, and Jesus silences this lack of faith as well as the storm itself."[7] Jesus, initially tranquilly asleep and then commanding the storm to cease, holds the venture together. He is the still point at the center that can hold the fear of drowning, and the fear of falling apart, and psychic fragmentation, and in a future boat journey contain the fear of the past returning to haunt.[8]

Joe explains how in his late twenties things began to feel as if they might fall apart again. He found it hard to go to work, and once there even harder to concentrate. He felt he had no purpose in life, that any meaning seemed to have left, and he had no idea who he really was. Everything went dark, gray at best, and he felt shrouded in darkness and despair that he could not seem to get out and under from. At his very lowest ebb and fearing his morbid feelings, he came across the Bible story of Jesus asleep in the boat while the night storm raged, and how then Jesus calmed everything down.

It happened when Joe had been waiting for several hours at a clinic to see a psychiatrist. The GP had referred him for an assessment. In the waiting room there was a table with some magazines, but when he looked all the magazines seemed to be about happy and successful people. On a shelf underneath the table, he found a

5. Myers, *Binding*, 197.

6. Malbon, *Narrative Space*, 78.

7. Myers, *Binding*, 196.

8. McGann, *Journeying Self*, 68.

Gideon's Bible. He said that he felt so bored and fed up with everything he thought he'd take a look at it. So he randomly opened the Bible and found the passage about the first sea crossing:

> Joe
>
> Of course, I wasn't religious—didn't go to church or anything like that, but this really blew my mind. I felt it was the strangest story to read—just as I felt I was drowning in misery. I thought it was a message to me—and actually I still believe that—crazy as it might sound. Then I thought that perhaps there *was* something out there that could help me—someone who could come to save me . . . Course much later I saw it wasn't quite like that—I had to do more work myself. But it was finding that bit of the Bible at that very moment when I was so desperate. I gabbled about all this with the psychiatrist, pouring everything out, and she suggested a therapy group once a week for a couple of months or so. So, I thought well why not? Nothing to lose. I had to wait a while, but then I began to go to the group meetings . . .
>
> I was very tense about it, but what made sense was that I just felt I couldn't try to recover on my own. I mean my mum and dad and sister were all trying to help, but they were worrying as much as me . . . I needed to depend on something or somebody to be there for me, and I guess this is what the group did. The group used ideas from the 12-Step programme, and we had a buddy scheme where each of us looked after another person too, offering support. The group ran on the idea, which I'd say now that it's like a mantra: "we can do together what we could not do alone"—and that's been so true.

Joe explained how the twelve-step program influenced the therapy group, which was for people who were depressed. They called it Depressed Anonymous (Joe referred to it as Depressives Anonymous), and adjusted the steps originally designed to tackle addictions to fit with depression.

Joe

> The first step is about admitting we are powerless—I felt I already knew that, but the thing is you have to get there before any healing can start. But then the second step turned out to fit with reading that Bible passage. Basically, it's about surrendering to a higher power—this whole thing I was getting into about blaming myself for not sorting myself out . . . No, it's about getting help. I wasn't sure who or what that higher power really was, but I was happy to go along with it. Sometimes it seemed like the group, other times it was as if something greater than me was guiding me along some path.

## FEAR OF DROWNING

Evie has shared how the old feelings of desolation, separation anxiety, hypervigilance, and catastrophic thinking began to take over in such a way that she knew she needed to seek help. Here was the hope that things might be different, but it came with much fear. Evie writes how almost immediately after starting psychotherapy she began to regress. This meant trying to keep functioning despite an uprush of the old symptoms that she'd developed as a child. Setting off on this night sea journeying was immediately turbulent, but she knew there would be no going back. She writes of the panics, feeling sick, and fear of falling apart that dominated the early months of the therapy.

Evie

> I went to the therapist I had contacted, and told her how I had been feeling desolate, all confused and very worried about my mother and how I might help mother and make her happier. I went through my childhood and after felt completely elated—I thought "I've done it now and I already feel so much better" . . . but then the next morning felt sick, panicky and very anxious—but worst of all I couldn't swallow and couldn't eat anything—I had

> to take the day off work as I felt so weird. I also had this dream that I was in a little Noddy toy car with this therapist, and we were travelling up a hill: on one side was a deep forest, and on the other side was the sea, and the waves were getting higher and higher, and I thought they might turn the car over—we were both getting so wet.
>
> When I told her all this the next week, and I couldn't really believe it myself, but I started to make myself sick before I went in to see her—I couldn't tell her that somehow—it made me look too odd and ill, she said all the physical stuff—not eating and being panicky was to do with keeping all the feelings down—repression, and then beginning to release them. She said it was like undoing a cork, and the drink fizzing over. She said the dream was setting the scene for the therapy that we would do together. At least, I thought, she's in the toy child's car with me . . . She suggested I try Complan, which is food in a drink—suddenly I was like a baby again. Luckily that didn't last too long. In the sessions I lay wrapped up in a blanket staring at her in case she left me. I really worried on top of all that about coping with work and the family—it began to feel very frightening, but once I'd started trying to sort out the past, I couldn't stop—or rather something inside me pushed me on and on, and it wasn't as if I could go back anyway!
>
> But the more I tried to talk about the past the more frightened I became, until in the end it seemed to be about survival. One day I was feeling so dreadful I just lay like a baby in a foetal position, just keeping breathing took over my whole body, it almost rocked me; my limbs were powerless. I felt I could stay curled up for a long time. But then I thought—my breathing is also spirit. I am alive. I am surviving. That was the worst but slowly, slowly I came out of that for the long slog.

As Evie began to work with an empathic therapist, she was getting a sense of what had really happened to her in the past. Over the weeks and months, the past trauma was being re-experienced in the present, but it could be thought about, talked about, and shared, and so eventually understood. Donald Winnicott writes about this fear of falling apart and drowning, which he sees as part of taking the person back to what he calls "an unthinkable state of affairs" and "primitive agonies."[9] He thought this state is the fear of a breakdown that has already happened. If a child has been traumatized, especially in infancy, then the experience of these agonies remains in the psyche, carried around hidden away in the unconscious, and the psyche develops defenses to keep the overwhelming anxiety under control.

The small child is not able to integrate what was happening at the time, and so the trauma remains ever present until it can be acknowledged, recognized, and experienced in the present. If the trauma happens when the child is very young then it cannot be properly verbalized, or even properly experienced, and so cannot get sufficiently integrated into the total personality. In other words, there was a failure of support by those looking after the child at a stage when support was indispensable for going-on-being and soul development.

The fear of falling apart or drowning is the fear of death—but a death that has already been gone through when the trauma felt like death to the child. This leaves the adult feeling that they could be annihilated, and once again back in touch with what happened long ago. Soul recovery needs the adult to accept that what they are feeling in the present is what they felt in the past. The difference is that the context has changed, and there are other strategies available to manage the emotions. Winnicott writes about getting "to the bottom of the trough" where what is so feared can be remembered in the sense that it can be properly experienced in the present.[10] From his professional and personal experiences Winnicott knew that the movement towards deep dependency and the fear of breakdown will reach a limit, from which spontaneous recovery and renewed health will follow: "He is the explorer who has been there and knows."[11]

9. Winnicott, "Fear of Breakdown," 103, 104.

10. Winnicott, "Fear of Breakdown," 103–7.

11. See Rodman, *Winnicott*, 301.

Night sea journeying takes courage as it's not only about confronting the damage that was experienced in childhood, but also about confronting oneself. In the first years of therapy Evie says that she kept feeling so overwhelmed by anxiety and panic that it almost felt as if she were possessed. It took a lot of energy to retain control of her emotions as they seemed so raw, but despite all this difficulty it was many years before she could really accept how bad things had been, and recognize how amazing it was that she had managed as well as she had.

Being completely overwhelmed is powerfully described by James V. Downton, who sets out on his inward night sea journeying, initially seeing a Jungian analyst for a midlife crisis. After five years of therapy, and when feeling more positive, Downton considered ending the work. But then everything suddenly changed:

> Expecting calm seas, I was completely caught off guard when . . . a great wave from the unconscious suddenly crashed over me. The wave pushed me into the depths of the night sea where a water monster was waiting to swallow me.[12]

Downton found that his fear and the power of what was emerging from his unconscious led him to a state of panic, and feeling "frightened, lost, and completely alone." His whole body felt taken over by a white heat, and with this his breathing became shallow, and at time he felt as if he were living in a fog. Throughout, and by a tremendous effort, he kept at his work as a university lecturer as well as following the routines of family life:

> But then darkness would come like a welcome time of sanctuary, when I was alone trying to grasp the deeper meaning of my dreams and to understand the origin and purpose of the white heat.[13]

An early dream seemed to offer a clear warning of the danger he felt of either going insane or dying:

12. Downton Jr., *Night Sea Journey*, 13.

13. Downton Jr., *Night Sea Journey*, 13.

> I'm at a lake where the water is turning a muddy colour. So I go to the top of a cliff surrounding the lake and throw a piece of blue colour into the water. When it hits the surface, the water turns a brilliant blue. Then I see a slide going down into the water. I'm told that going down the slide is extremely dangerous because once a teenage boy went so far under the water that he almost drowned.[14]

As a way of dealing with the fear, Downton eventually shared what was happening with his wife, and began reading Carl Jung. One of the things he read about was Jung's own experiment with night sea journeying. Jung's inner need to resolve parts of his own childhood trauma and free himself from unfinished business with both his parents and his work as a psychiatrist, initially led him to self-analysis and his work with Sigmund Freud. After the break with Freud, Jung lost his status within the psychoanalytic community and also some of his work; his reputation was tarnished, and he found himself isolated, disorientated, and alone. As quoted at the start of chapter 2, Jung set out to rediscover his soul, and the lost world linked to his childhood. Jung began his night sea journey by allowing himself to drop into his deep unconscious and rediscover his soul:

> I was sitting at my desk once more, thinking over my fears. Then I let myself drop. Suddenly it was as though the ground literally gave way beneath my feet, and I plunged down into dark depths. I could not fend off a feeling of panic.[15]

For Jung this was a creative illness that became the inspiration for his later work, a new psychology for the cure of souls. "The years when I was pursuing my inner images were the most important in my life—in them everything essential was decided . . . a lifetime's work." He wrote about a treasure hidden in the deep unconscious, a treasure that is hard to attain, and as the shining pearl, is in part a mystery. It was this treasure that Jung set out to

14. Downton Jr., *Night Sea Journeying*, 13.

15. Jung, *Memories, Dreams and Reflections*, 203.

find. He believed that when properly understood, the mental suffering involved is ultimately transcended because it brings insight, vision, and understanding.[16]

## THE HEALING ON THE OTHER SIDE OF THE SEA OF GALILEE

In Mark's Gospel, a powerful healing takes place immediately as the boat arrives safely on the other side of the lake. It is as if the outer storm with the wind and water is replaced by an inner storm of powerful emotional psychodynamics that are similarly uncontrollable and wild. In the boat Jesus has subdued the elemental energies, on land he frees the energies locked up in a man possessed by dark and destructive forces. In the long account of Jesus liberating the man from his trauma, Mark gives us details of the man's symptoms: uncontrollable violence, self-harm, and howling in deep distress. The victim is utterly helpless and out of control, seemingly beyond any aid from others, and beyond any attempts to restrain him.

He is in the dark night of total abandonment, and his very self has fragmented into destructiveness. He stones and abuses himself, and is regularly chained by the community because of his insanity. Yet, this same man while in a psychotic state runs to Jesus, irresistibly drawn to his presence. In his fear, the man asks Jesus: "What have you to do with me, Jesus, Son of the Most High God? I adjure you by God, do not torment me."[17] Incidentally, this is the same question that is asked earlier in Mark by another emotionally troubled soul.[18]

Various biblical interpretations suggest the question is one of mockery, and the use of Jesus' name is an attempt to take control; however, by seeing the adult man's behavior as the result of a terribly abused childhood, it is possible to see instead the hidden soul

16. Jung, *Memories, Dreams and Reflections*, 178–79, 191.
17. Mark 5:7.
18. Mark 1:24.

reacting to Jesus' presence, longing for healing and connection, and begging for no further traumatization. The "demons" are the internal oppressors based on the past, but that still powerfully possess the adult man, and that often have been projected out, so that his past ill treatment is repeated endlessly in the present both by the man himself and by the villagers. The ill man is overwhelmed by conflict, tension, and fear—repressing his hatred and mixed feelings for what has happened to him, and then erupting into self-loathing and self-harm. The power of his distress both frightens and excites those who see him. All are caught in a cycle of abuse and re-abuse.

Jesus takes control and commands the damaging spirits to leave. Here is Jesus' ministry of liberation: having been named, seen, and acknowledged by Jesus, the destructive emotions that had taken over the man, and indeed his local community, are now reintegrated back into the unconscious. In a highly symbolic gesture, they are returned to the unconscious by infecting a herd of pigs and drowning them in the water. In psychological jargon it could be said that the ego, the rational part of the man, has now been re-established to the fore of his psyche, and the irrational is eased and brought back under control. This rebirth, indeed almost a resurrection of the innocent child part of the man, shocks the community, which seems more afraid of this healing than the original status quo. Of course, the grateful man, like the healed child that he is, longs to stay with Jesus and be with him all the time; instead, Jesus enjoins the man to accept his freedom as a gift, to go home, and to be with those who will love him. The man leaves, speaking of God's loving kindness and mercy, and so demonstrating the recovery of his soul to everyone.

Jesus shows deep understanding and compassion towards this tormented man, an understanding probably deepened by Jesus' own experience earlier in Mark 3:21–27, when he too is threatened by a form of restraint, and accused of being possessed by satanic forces. The heart of Jesus' mission is not to deny or crush by power, but rather to recognize, confront, and transform. The night sea journeying involves the eventual acceptance of all the shadow parts of ourselves that we would rather not look at, let alone accept; all has to be seen and acknowledged, especially the parts of ourselves that feel so unlovable, disgusting, and hateful.

## "WHAT HAVE YOU TO DO WITH ME, JESUS?"

This question asked by the tormented man, roaming amongst the tombstones and the twilight world of the dead, is central. Therapeutic insights are important, therapeutic support and guidance helpful, but for real change to happen there needs to be a change of vision: a spiritual awakening. An example of this is shown in a letter to Carl Jung written by William (Bill) G. Wilson, co-founder of Alcoholics Anonymous. In the early 1930s a patient of Jung's, Roland H., stopped drinking during his analysis, but relapsed soon afterwards. He returned to Jung, asking to resume the analysis to help him to become abstinent once again. Jung refused, telling him bluntly that nothing less than exposing himself to the experience of a genuine religious conversion could be effective—and that even that might fail.

Roland H. was utterly shocked, but the refusal pushed him to rock bottom. Returning to the US, he joined the Oxford Group, which had helped many alcoholics to become sober. Within this group he did undergo a religious conversion, and he became sober. It was in part his influence that led to the co-founding of Alcoholics Anonymous in 1934. As Wilson wrote to Jung in 1961, "This astonishing chain of events actually started long ago in your consulting room, and it was directly founded upon your own humility and deep perception."[19]

In his reply, Jung, pleased to find out what had happened to his ex-patient, writes: "His craving for alcohol was the equivalent on a low level of the spiritual thirst of our being for wholeness, expressed in medieval language: the union with God." Jung links this to: "As the hart panteth after the water brooks, so panteth my

19. Wilson, "Bill W. Carl Jung Letters."

soul after thee, O God."[20] In his reply to Wilson, Jung reflects that recovery happens when walking on a path that leads to higher understanding. We might be led through grace, or through personal and honest contact with friends, or "through a high education of the mind beyond the confines of mere rationalism." Jung writes that he is convinced that:

> the evil principle prevailing in this world leads the unrecognized spiritual need into perdition, if it is not counteracted either by a real religious insight or by the protective wall of human community. An ordinary man, not protected by an action from above and isolated in society, cannot resist the power of evil . . . Alcohol in Latin is spiritus and you use the same word for the highest religious experience as well as the most depraving poison. The helpful formula therefore is: *spiritus contra spiritum*.[21]

In other words, high spirit against low spirit. For every human being is a spiritual being, and the concern is whether the spirituality is self-destructive and isolating, or positive and life-giving. As if to emphasize Jung's approach on the importance of religious ideas and convictions in the recovery from emotional conflict, he replies in another letter to an Irish monk who asked whether Jung still stood by his claim that "among all my patients in the second half of life . . . none . . . has been really healed who did not regain his religious outlook." Jung writes:

> Religious ideas and convictions from the beginning of history . . . represent the world of wholeness in which fragments can be gathered and put together again. Such a cure cannot be effected by pills and injections.[22]

20. Psalm 42:1.
21. Jung, *Letters* 2, 623–25.
22. Jung, *Letters* 2, 625.

# 6

# Riding the Waves

When winds are raging o'er the upper ocean
And billows wild contend with angry roar,
'Tis said, far down, beneath the wild commotion
That peaceful stillness reigneth evermore.[1]

## MARK'S DESCRIPTION OF THE SECOND SEA VOYAGE WHERE JESUS IS SEEN WALKING ON THE WATER AND GETTING INTO THE BOAT WITH THE DISCIPLES

Immediately he made his disciples get into the boat and go on ahead to the other side, to Bethsaida, while he dismissed the crowd. After saying farewell to them, he went up on the mountain to pray.

When evening came, the boat was out on the lake, and he was alone on the land. When he saw that they were straining at the oars against an adverse wind, he came towards them early in the morning, walking on the lake. He intended to pass them by. But when they saw him walking on the lake, they thought it was a ghost

1. Harriet Beecher Stowe, cited in Hill, *Dangerous Prayers*, 167.

> and cried out; for they all saw him and were terrified. But immediately he spoke to them and said, "Take heart, it is I; do not be afraid." Then he got into the boat with them and the wind ceased. And they were utterly astounded, for they did not understand about the loaves, but their hearts were hardened.[2]

On this second crossing, the disciples are compelled to make the journey on their own. It is only toward daybreak that Jesus comes to help, but leaving the disciples terrified and apprehensive. This voyage takes place straight after the miracle of the feeding of the five thousand with five loaves and two fishes, and when the journey is over, there is an account of mass healings of those who rushed about to bring the sick to Jesus, begging that "they might touch even the fringe of his cloak; and all who touched it were healed."[3] The voyage and the mass encounters that are described before and after the sea voyage are about aspects of relationships: needing connection with others and the nurturance it brings; doubting relationship and being frightened by it; and also having faith in the power of a relationship to heal and change things.

Getting close to people, testing out relationships, and allowing dependency and vulnerability are all risky ventures for those who have experienced adverse childhood experiences. Night sea journeying takes the person on a roller coaster of emotions. This description linked to developing what is called "a surfer mentality" could be helpful in thinking about what can get stirred up:

> The boat sits on the ocean; sometimes still, sometimes bobbing gently, sometimes on the point of sinking. The sea is the sea and the boat is the boat, they don't change, yet the conditions surrounding them vary immensely. It's pretty unlikely the boat will always remain still and equally unlikely that it will always move so violently as to nearly capsize. Conditions change, time passes, in cycles, lows and highs—the journey; a journey of swings.

2. Mark 6:45–52.
3. Mark 6:56b.

### *RIDING THE WAVES*

> Life can sometimes be like riding the waves in a sail boat—occasionally you get to steer and choose your course, sometimes balance, sometimes ripples. Temporary situations; moments of turbulence and times of stillness. Occasionally you need to cast out the anchor and wait, other times you need to pull up the anchor and drift, not always knowing the destination. Occasionally the tide takes you or the wind blows and you have to go with the flow. Now and then the wind calms and you can gently float, reassess and contemplate.[4]

In this chapter, issues of trust, faith, and dependency are explored. Relationships with those who might help soul recovery from trauma are discussed, and ghosts from the past who seem to be hindering soul recovery are acknowledged. Inevitably night sea journeying brings up much unfinished business from childhood that has been kept below the surface. Part of the unfinished business involves relationships.

## "O GOD, THY SEA IS SO GREAT AND MY BOAT IS SO SMALL"[5]—LEARNING TO TRUST AGAIN

Quite quickly on the night sea journey the person who has been traumatized as a child is required to face up to their feelings of vulnerability—feelings that have often been hidden for decades, avoided and protected by symptoms. To do this there needs to be an ally or allies, and connection to something or someone attractive or interesting, something or someone physically, emotionally, and/or spiritually present. But, how to allow this to happen?

> I trusted, even when I said:
> "I am sorely afflicted,"
> And when I said in my alarm:
> "There is no one I can trust."[6]

4. Mind Map Inspiration, "Riding the Waves," paras. 1–2.
5. Opening to an old Breton prayer.
6. Psalm 116:10, as rendered in Johnson, ed., *Benedictine Daily Prayer*.

The psalmist perfectly captures here the dilemma for the person who was traumatized as a child. We need to trust even if our faith in trusting another person previously has been upsetting and damaging, and we remain wary. Healing needs trust and belief—healing takes place in relationship, and can only be effective if trust develops in the relationship. In Mark's account, the role Jesus plays in this development of trust is central. Leaving the disciples to travel alone, Jesus sets out to pray, and yet, he is also present as a watcher of what is happening on the sea journey, and witness to the difficulties for his companions as, once again, they battle against the wind and unruly water.

However, Jesus is not only a witnessing presence here, but on seeing their distress, he changes his intention to merely observe, or "to pass them by," and, instead speaks to reassure the fearful men, and wonderfully gets right into the boat with them. Then the wind stops, and the journey continues calmly. Here for the disciples, as often for us too, there is need, doubt, and faith all in the one encounter. This pattern of need, doubt, and faith: we need someone trustworthy to listen to us; our previous experience leads us to doubt this possibility; and we have to hold to even the smallest amount of faith that something might be different this time.

Opening up the inner world brings the realization that things are not well, and the further realization that to open up will involve vulnerability, learning to trust again and to be in relationship. The loss of trust as a result of trauma has to be gradually reinstated so the person can restore their sense of self, and sense of self-worth in the context of being a part of humanity in authentic relation with others. Our sense of self, of self-worth, of humanity, depends on a feeling of connection with others. This may involve allowing a dependency to develop on another person, and it is through such dependence that there can come an understanding of the effect of the most significant people from childhood, and the quality of the relationship with them—both good and bad.

Evie's dependency on her therapist developed very quickly and during an early holiday break from her therapy, she describes in her diary how anxious she is, and how much she has placed her trust and faith in the therapist.

> Evie
>
> I get panicky, no strength in me and then feeling there's no strength in anyone around me . . . If I think of strength; I think of her [the analyst]. I wonder what she's doing, did she like the card I gave her before her holiday, should I have used different words and then her words to me—"don't lose yourself!" When I'm out in town or going to work I find I'm looking out for her, even though I know she's away. In the end I wrote all the days she was away on a card and crossed them off, like a prisoner longing for the day of their release.

When the sessions started up again after the holiday, Evie was able to discuss how vulnerable she had felt, and the therapist linked this back to what Evie had felt as a small child when she had been fostered during one of her mother's illnesses. Evie could feel in the present an old, odd feeling that she had been too young to put into words and understand. It was a mixture of panic at being left, anger at what had happened, and a deep longing for everything to feel safe. At the same time as being in therapy, Evie was testing out her openness to God by spending time each evening meditating and praying. She found herself sharing with God how lost she felt at times, and asking whether Jesus, who knew about being abandoned and feeling lost, could help. She began to feel more secure from this time apart, able to speak without feeling judged, and so some of the anxieties could be spoken of and held in the silence. As this evening routine became established, Evie found this increasingly helpful, and a way of repairing some of her lack of trust and faith. Kevin Fauteux, writer and therapist, acknowledges the potential of a regular time with God:

> The experience of a God who walks through the valley of a person's fears has the potential to make the person feel safe enough to confront the trepidation that originally

> made him fear walking on his own and so seek refuge in God.[7]

Soul recovery can involve moving away from a false pseudo-independence to re-experiencing genuine dependency, where the dependency is on something more than ourselves, and that can begin to bring comfort. As explored in an earlier chapter, some children sense a divine presence alongside them in their traumatic suffering, and as the night sea journeying begins in adulthood, this same presence may reappear—a light that guides, a presence within, a divine child at the center of our very being willing us into becoming the person that we are meant to be, and whose development was so interrupted. Starting to feel a dependency on God—a bit like the developing dependency on a therapist—allows the person to begin to grow, and to emotionally open to the parts that have been so damaged and stunted. It is the beginning of ending our spiritual estrangement and exile, and accepting a state of being-in-dependency with God. As with Evie, here Jesus Christ can be an intercessory figure, able to bridge the compartmentalized self.

The psychoanalyst James Grotstein refers to the lost part of ourselves, our soul, as an innocent self that is being held hostage by the past: "*the most holy aspect of ourselves*, the innocent self that we sold into bondage and left in the embrace of the dark demon." He describes someone who had a history of trauma as a child and who had been stuck in his therapy for years,

> complaining bitterly of his fate as a neglected and abandoned child, utterly unable to find any gratitude in his life for anything, including his analysis. While on vacation in France the patient visited the Cathedral de la Sacre Coeur and reported a religious experience there. Gazing upon the statue of Christ, who seemed to reach out for him mercifully and forgivingly, the patient exclaimed, "I don't need psychoanalysis! I need God in order to regain my innocence."[8]

7. Fauteux, *Recovery of the Self*, 156.
8. Grotstein, *Who is the Dreamer*, 182, 222.

As a traumatized child, Thomas Merton knew about soul recovery through spiritual dependency, where our knowledge of God is nothing to do with an object that we look at, but rather comes from our personal experience of "ourselves as utterly dependent on his saving and merciful knowledge of us."[9] Existing within this dependence, we are carried by God as we journey across the night sea. For Thomas Merton spiritual recovery became a long process of increasing dependency, intimacy, and union with Christ. This growing awareness of dependency, then, is part of what it means to become integrated.

One image that takes us right back to infancy is of connection with the breast of God, as an infant nursing, where the person is less and less conscious of self as a separate thing. Once spiritual dependency is allowed, then there is the accompanying realization of the deepest of realities—the infinite fragility of the divine life in us. Merton writes of the weakness and littleness of this in each one of us, which is fortunately indestructible. He sees this as a mustard seed, and as the struggle of the very small to survive. The true self is like a "shy wild animal" that can only emerge when "all is peaceful, in silence . . . alone."[10] Following his conversion Merton writes:

> For I was now, at last, born: but I was still only new-born. I was living: I had an interior life, real, but feeble and precarious. And I was still nursed and fed with spiritual milk. . . . The life of grace had at last, it seemed, become constant, permanent. Weak and without strength as I was, I was nevertheless walking in the way that was liberty and life.[11]

The struggle is to become open to the process of rebirth and renewal, despite the fear of what we might find within us. Lessening our compulsive attachment to the symptoms protecting us from past trauma can be helped by a belief that we are not alone in the suffering, that we are being held in a loving and kind way.

9. Merton, *Contemplative Prayer*, 103–4.
10. Merton, *Inner Experience*, 5.
11. Merton, *Seven Storey Mountain*, 332.

## GHOSTS FROM THE PAST

At the beginning of the night's third watch,
before there is moonlight,
Don't be surprised to meet yet not recognize
What is surely a familiar face from the past.[12]

As our hearts soften, disembodied specters from the past have to be confronted and dealt with so that they can become integrated. This part of the chapter looks at how the internal oppressor(s) can be brought into a manageable form. In Mark's account of Jesus walking on the water toward the frightened disciples, Jesus is initially seen not as the loved teacher, but as a ghost—something frightening and possibly malevolent. Jesus appears in the final hours of the night, in the liminal time between night and day. The disciples seeing this figure respond out of fear and not faith. He is in their minds an apparition, a spirit of the night heralding disaster, a soul or malignant spirit of a dead person.

The disciples could have instead seen him as a divine manifestation who walks on water (whereas ghosts do not), but in their misunderstanding and terror they reduce Jesus to something impossible from their collective past history. When Jesus reassures them, the walking on the water becomes an epiphany, where fear is confronted and self-belief is re-established. "Take heart, it is I; do not be afraid." In their relief the disciples open themselves to his presence as he joins them on the sea voyage, and all becomes safe.

One insight from this account is that even what feels most chaotic and irrational in ourselves can be made sense of, and managed by developing a deepening trust, faith, and relationship in God and others. Another insight is that something beyond our previously learned experiences may come to us in times of fear, offering a new way of looking at and thinking about the world. "I believe; help my unbelief!"[13] In the context of soul recovery fol-

12. Tung-tiang Cheh, in Fauteux, *Recovery of the Self*, 67.

13. Mark 9:24.

lowing childhood trauma the adult may become easily reminded, or triggered, by someone in the present who reminds them of a traumatizing person from the past. This was Joe's experience.

Joe

Well, during the group therapy something important came up, and that sort of changed things. What happened was at the start I was finding the group really helpful in raising my mood, and I began to come out of the depression I'd been stuck in for what seemed like years. I really looked forward to the group each week. I thought the person who ran it was great—he was kind, funny, and also smart . . . He didn't say much, but somehow held together the whole thing—especially when people got upset or cross with each other. We were loosely following the 12-Step programme for Depressives Anonymous and I wasn't yet sure what I understood by God, but to tell the truth I thought this guy who led it, Matt, was a bit god-like himself, and I found I was trusting him. Then there were the steps about making "a searching and fearless moral inventory of ourselves" and "admitting to God, to ourselves and to another human being the exact nature of our wrongs."[14] This was Step Five, and I wasn't sure I wanted to go there or how to, but it seemed most of the others did.

But then I began to feel the group was going wrong for me, and I thought I'd stop going. I hadn't said that much generally, though I liked listening to others, but when I did say something, I thought people weren't that interested. I thought perhaps I wasn't as smart as the others, or interesting enough, or even depressed enough! But then one of the women one week completely ignored me, when I had actually said something, she pretended she hadn't heard. The aim of the group is to be a community who share our experiences week by week, the ups and the downs so we help each other to recover from depression and stop saddening ourselves. I'm repeating that just in case you too didn't hear—the group was about helping

14. Depressed Anonymous, "12 Steps."

each other, and stop saddening ourselves. This bastard woman was making me feel just rubbish—hating myself and hating her . . . I thought who the fuck did she think she was ignoring me, and not seeing me at all.

So, I told Matt I couldn't hack the meetings, and they were making me feel worse . . . but he said I should try and hang on in there and bring it up. Before the next group I was bricking it—I felt like throwing up, really worried about saying something—and then when I did, it all sort of blurted out—like saying to her, and really everyone "why don't you like me . . . don't you want me here?" It was all full on, but then this woman didn't seem to know what I was talking about and was shocked. Anyway, it all went on, and then someone said—"hey man, I know where you're coming from—this is about rejection—who's rejected you and hurt you so much." And then I cried—I NEVER cry, but I did and couldn't stop. I said about being adopted and about my birth mother—I was someone who had been given away—someone who wasn't wanted. My adoptive parents told me I was specially chosen by them, but it still left the truth of not being good enough for the first mother, and then not looked after enough by the foster mother—OMG it all spilt out. After people were hugging me, and I felt like I'd let go of something, but wasn't sure what . . .

What we all worked out was that thinking that the woman—Jan—was rejecting me had started up a whole association which I'd been holding inside me—well all my life. That I was no good because my mother didn't want me. It felt an absolute revelation, and I could see how I'd avoided putting myself out there too much—not just in the group, but in all sorts of other ways as well in case I got rejected. And that's especially around women. The nice bit was that in the meeting Jan explained she hadn't known she was ignoring me, but she was just wrapped up in her own stuff. Later she gave me a hug, and said it had been an important meeting for her too, helping her to appreciate that when she got lost inside herself it was affecting others too.

The idea of confessing to another person, or as for Joe with the group, is a deeply powerful experience, and a difficult one. We can go through the motions of explaining or talking about things, but to be in touch with all the associated feelings in an authentic way is totally different. As Edward Sellner writes about Step Five: "The fact is that most of us find it extremely difficult to be honest with ourselves, let alone someone else. Deep down we're afraid of what might happen if we did open up." Yet, as Sellner himself learned, nothing can change unless we acknowledge and accept it first. "Self-knowledge and self-acceptance depend upon telling our story, being heard by someone other than ourselves—and, perhaps most importantly, hearing ourselves speak."[15]

Confronting this tendency for the past to intrude repeatedly in the present is an important part of night sea journeying. In the myths about such journeys the hero deals with various dangerous sea monsters who threaten him or her by reducing them to size, and then moving on. The idea of being devoured by a monster from the deep is particularly relevant to those who have been traumatized in childhood, and is closely connected with significant adults entwining, insinuating themselves, and taking over both our inner and often external world. It is hard to break free.

In the myth of night sea journeying as recounted by the ethnologist Leo Frobenius, the hero has to defy all the danger and descend into the belly of the monster—the journey into hell, and stay there for some time—night sea imprisonment. In some versions, three days is the term used for night sea imprisonment: the time Christ spent in the underworld, and Jonah spent in the belly of the whale. It is also the time of the three darkest days of the year—December 21 to 24. Inside the monster, the hero seeks for a way to get free, in some myths by lighting a fire inside, so that in the very place of death, the spark of life is secretly being created. As the monster is destroyed it drifts to land, where the hero once more sees daylight. The struggle is to disentangle the present from the past, and ego consciousness from the grip of the unconscious. Rebecca Parker describes this as a battle between good and evil:

15. Sellner, *Step 5*, 2–3.

> This was the force of the abuser in my life. He occupied the place of God. It was his presence, his will, his actions that ruled my life. I had no other god before him. My spirit bowed down to him. I accepted that I was who he said I was. His spirit filled my life. . . . I began to think of my struggle as a struggle with idolatry . . . Where the relationship with the abuser was an unholy alliance.[16]

If a person has caused the child trauma their image remains stuck in the survivor's psyche, often acting as a powerful force not only against authentic feeling, but imprisoning the child, later the adult, with chains of guilt, criticism, and responsibility. The child often carries all the pain of what has happened. For survivors of childhood trauma unlocking the chains from the past is complex, because we often find ourselves back in a similar situation. Perhaps there is a hope that this time the outcome could be different, or perhaps there's an attempt to master the situation. The difficulty is that the pattern of the past trauma can get reinforced by a recurrence in adulthood. This is what happened to James Finley.

As discussed in chapter 4, Finley felt consoled by God as a child, and his faith in God sustained him in the midst of the family trauma that was ongoing. This faith deepened in adolescence through his reading of Thomas Merton, which led him to the idea of joining a monastery. Despite threats from his violent father, Finley finished high school, walked out of his family home, and went to the Abbey of Gethsemani. When asked at the interview about psychological difficulties, Finley said there were none.

> In one sense I lied in telling him this because I was afraid that if I told him about the trauma and the ways it had affected me, he would not give permission for me to enter the monastery. And I felt so strongly that God was calling me to the monastic life that I felt I had a right to at least try it. At a more interior level I answered this way because I had been so deeply traumatized since I was a

16. Brock and Parker, *Proverbs of Ashes*, 195.

> small child that I did not know I was traumatized. My fear-based traumatized self was my normal self.[17]

Initially, Finley found consolation and strength through the monastic training and practices, but over time the fear from childhood re-emerged in overwhelming anxiety about being called on in one of the classes. Overcoming this fear, Finley moved to become a novice with Thomas Merton. On first meeting Merton, Finley felt so inadequate in front of this famous monk that he began to hyperventilate, and was too nervous to speak coherently. Merton, seeing Finley's extreme anxiety, asked him to come to his office every day to tell Merton one thing that had happened to Finley while he was working at the pig barn. This worked.

> Out of everything I have learned from prayerfully exploring Thomas Merton's teachings over the years, nothing has affected me more deeply than the wisdom and compassion in which he, in hearing me say, "I am afraid because you are Thomas Merton," responded in such a simple and compassionate way and allowed me to feel relaxed and comfortable in his presence. In this way he freed me up to share with him the sincere longing for God that drew me into the monastery.[18]

This lovely example of Merton helping Finley develop trust and faith is sadly contrasted with a later experience in the monastery, where a spiritual confessor groomed and sexually abused Finley. This was someone with whom Finley shared his traumatic past, but who then sexualized this trust. The dilemma for all traumatized children, which is that the child cannot survive without the parent who is destroying them, was re-enacted for Finley as an adult. A ghost/monster from the past had returned, which took Finley back to childhood, but now with the added horrible realization that there was nowhere to escape from the trauma, either physically or psychologically.

17 Finley, *Healing Path*, 38–39.

18. Finley, *Healing Path*, 65.

> [There was] no place so pure and innocent as a cloistered monastery, that traumatizing forces could not find me and bring me down. This was especially devastating for me in realizing that I was passively going along with the destructive forces that were bringing me down . . . It seemed that just as my passivity traumatically bonded me to my father, so, too, my passivity traumatically bonded me to the priest.[19]

Finley raises the question of the extent that the intensity of traumatizing events can limit our experiential access to God's sustaining presence. "The grace lies in the ways in which the light of God's presence begins to shine ever so meekly in the darkness in which we have lost our way."[20] Release comes in holding on to the grace through the cycle between the good times and the bad times, the insights and the return to the patterns that originally damaged us. This is grace that deepens with each experience, until our confidence in the light is stronger that our fear of the darkness. Finley left the monastery he had lived in for nearly six years, but writes that it took another twenty years before he could really be healed from his fear of being true to himself in the midst of his own life. The power of past patterns of behaving, and the strength needed to break the patterns can easily be underestimated.

## RIDING THE WAVES

Deep calls to deep
at the thunder of your cataracts
all your waves and your billows
have gone over me.[21]

Ye eternal Trinity, our deep sea into which the more I enter the more I find and the more I find the more I seek,

19. Finley, *Healing Path*, 80.
20. Finley, *Healing Path*, 85.
21. Psalm 42:7.

our eternal Godhead what more could you give me than yourself.[22]

In the Bible there is much symbolism around the perilous sea where drowning can symbolize being lost or damned. The prayer by Catherine of Siena, quoted above, offers another way of looking at what might be found in deep sea. For what is needed during night sea journeying is not about deliverance from the danger of the sea, but rather about finding a way of being alive in the depths. There is then a transforming of what is found in the depths by bringing it up to the surface. In John 21:6 Jesus helped the fishermen make a good catch, and now invites us to fish around for what sea monsters we might find and bring into the boat to land on the seashore.

There are the good times too, for as the waves take the adult traumatized as a child down into the depths—so the movement raises them up again. The pendulum swings the other way. This is about riding the waves. Evie describes how sometimes she would wryly wonder how it can be called getting better when it felt so terrible. Then after a particularly bad few days of anxiety and catastrophic thinking, she wrote in her diary how she was overwhelmed by the most wonderful, amazing, emotional, beautiful feelings.

Evie

> At the end of the road going down to the city center I was thinking of God, and then saw the spires of three churches in the town shimmering above a pink-grey morning mist. Above there were birds and the sun, and I was filled with the utter beauty of the whole thing—it was like the first morning—seeing creation for the first time—so much beauty. I laughed and that's when I realized that I wasn't alone with what I was going through, and there were consolations.

22. Catherine of Siena, *Dialogue*, 358.

When the Israelite prisoners are in exile and far from home, they ask the prophet twice, using the term "night watchman" or "sentinel," how long they have to endure the night. How much of the night has gone, and how much more is still to come. The plaintive cry is "Sentinel, what of the night? Sentinel, what of the night?"[23] This has been interpreted as when will this time of darkness, chaos, and difficulty end, and when will better times come?[24] The answer is that the morning will come, but then there will be other nights and other mornings: "Morning comes, and also the night. If you will inquire, inquire; come back again." One time of oppression will come to an end and there is release, but then another will come along and the cycle continues. Another interpretation is that the time of darkness will end, but it is uncertain whether there can be permanent relief, or perhaps a monster has been eluded, yet also not finally defeated. Creative clarity will come from the dark waters of chaos, but there will remain an undertow—not everything rises to the surface. The message from the prophet is to continue seeking and inquiring. Through this comes hope and encouragement, and where the significance and meaning in night sea seeking is understood as to do with the journeying, and not necessarily with the destination.

23. Isaiah 21:11–12.

24. Geyer, "Night of Dumah," 320, 330.

# 7

# Clear Waters

Precious Lord, take my hand,
lead me on, let me stand.
I am tired, I am weak, I am worn;
through the storm, through the night,
lead me on to the light:
take my hand, precious Lord lead me
home.[1]

THIS CHAPTER IS ABOUT the process of opening up awareness and understanding of what happened in childhood, and managing our responses as adults in a less destructive and a more helpful manner. It is about the way that night sea journeying eventually brings us into the increasing light of consciousness. A third sea journey from Mark's Gospel is used to explore this shift. This time the danger is not coming from outside the boat—from a storm or from fear of a ghost—but rather from inside the boat, and from the rigid way the disciples are thinking, or, rather, are *not* able to think about what has happened and what is happening to them. The accounts offer helpful ways of thinking about how as adults a traumatizing childhood can be processed, and to some extent integrated by the person leading to soul recovery.

1. Thomas Dorsey in Hill, *Dangerous Prayers*, 59.

After finishing the three months of group work based on Depressed Anonymous (DA, which Joe refers to as Depressives Anonymous), Joe shared that he had felt at a bit of a loose end. He joined a monthly support group of DA, but missed the intensity of the weekly meetings, and the wise advice from Matt. In the monthly group, one of the guys had been talking about bodywork and yoga, and so Joe decided to find a local yoga class—which he did.

Joe

> Over time with yoga, I found I could feel more at home in my body—I stopped feeling as if I was holding my breath, or holding myself together. I stopped feeling so bad about how I looked. Yoga became the real game-changer physically, and oddly it opened up my thinking and my feelings too. It was like my body became alive again. I really liked the teacher. An older guy called Andy—he was smallish too, but strong and had a confidence and calmness that I envied. But he was also welcoming, and sometimes after class we chatted for a while. It was odd as I can't remember how it came up, but he told me that he'd recently being trying to find out who his father was—apparently his mum had been a single parent, but he'd never known about his dad, and as a child he hadn't liked to ask, but eventually his mum's cousin mentioned his father had been an American based in the UK. Anyway, it got me thinking about whether I wanted to find out who my biological parents were . . . I mean I'd had the birth certificate with my biological mother's name, but didn't know anything much about her, and I hadn't liked to ask too in case it upset Mum and Dad, oh, and part of me wasn't sure I wanted to know.
>
> Long story short—and believe me—it was a long, long story as it took ages to get anywhere, but I did discover a bit. All my thinking—pretty negative too about my early years—well some was right about the shitty foster parent, but it turned out from the adoption file that the first placement had been okay, but then I had to be removed from the second when I became under-weight,

and had not had enough stimulation, that was the famous "failure to thrive" label. It was all in the file that I was small physically and pretty subdued; apparently, I just sat on this sofa wetting myself, with a dummy stuck in my mouth, watching telly, and not really much good at walking or talking. Then I got adopted and my development proper started up, thanks to Mum and Dad. The big surprise—I'd always thought my biological mother was some sort of—well—I won't say the word, but I'd thought the worst . . . It turned out she'd been on a gap year in Sri Lanka working at some charity project, and she'd got pregnant—it sounded like she'd liked the guy—but his family sort of blamed her, and he couldn't leave, and she had to come home to go to college or something, her parents wouldn't support her and she felt too young to have a kid on her own. So, I'm half Sri Lankan not Indian, there was a lot to adjust to about that. It was all there in black and white, and it needed a lot of thinking about. I did get some counseling when I was going through all this, and I talked about it a lot with Andy.

But it was the yoga that really opened me up with all the postures—asanas, and the breathing—pranayama, and the meditation. I began to take it seriously and decided after a while to train as a yoga teacher too. I did a course with the organization that Andy was part of. It wasn't about talking, but it was finally me listening to my body, and getting it right for me. I stopped feeling weird about how I looked, and after I'd thought about the file and who my birth parents were, I let it go—I didn't want to meet them, but I did want to concentrate on yoga and how my body felt in the moment—out of my head away from the past, and just as much as possible in the present moment. I liked the way I could choose what postures to do in my own practice, and, for how long. I began to feel empowered by it all, and oh so much better than before.

Perhaps you might think it a bit crazy, spending my time moving my body around in various positions, and adding the chanting from a long-dead language, but I felt I was coming home to something, being real, and wow dare I say it, a bit happier. It was being mindful, and it helped me feel clearer about my story. I realized that for

> about ten years I had just been stuck—a bit like me as a toddler—stuck on the sofa not walking or talking or having enough to eat—a bit sunk in misery, and the group stuff and the yoga began to shift all that.

The work with Depressed Anonymous, and especially taking up yoga, helped Joe widen his understanding of himself, and what had led to feeling so low and hopeless. He got a new perspective, and could begin to see more clearly how to live, and become the person he was meant to be, which included appreciating the impact the trauma had had on him. What the yoga offered was a developing awareness of what happens between the mind, the body, and the breath, and how the long-standing tension of the old trauma could gradually become unraveled. The memories were all stored in the body, even in the muscles and tissues, and focusing on the breath helped to get rid of some of this, as well as practicing the actual movements. The teacher of radical yoga Sandra Sabatini explains the importance of being aware of the breath.

> Breath is the key that can open thousands of doors—an infinitesimal but incredibly powerful laser capable of removing layers of encrustation. To experience this is very often like being on the crest of an oceanic wave, a simultaneous feeling of resistance and delight. . . . As the body is allowed to find its alignment between earth and sky, the practice becomes a richly rewarding voyage inwards where gifts are always offered with great generosity.[2]

## JESUS' TEACHING TO THE DISCIPLES ON THE THIRD SEA JOURNEY

The sea voyage we'll now discuss takes place after a second mass feeding miracle and more questioning from the Pharisees. Immediately after the journey, a blind man is healed on the second attempt.

2. Sabatini, *Breath*, 13.

> Now the disciples had forgotten to bring any bread; and they had only one loaf with them in the boat. And he cautioned them, saying, "Watch out—beware of the yeast of the Pharisees and the yeast of Herod." They said to one another, "It is because we have no bread." And becoming aware of it, Jesus said to them "Why are you talking about having no bread? Do you still not perceive or understand? Are your hearts hardened? Do you have eyes and fail to see? Do you have ears and fail to hear? And do you not remember? When I broke the five loaves for the five thousand, how many baskets full of broken pieces did you collect?" They said to him, "Twelve." "And the seven for the four thousand?" "Seven." Then he said to them, "Do you not yet understand?"[3]

For the disciples the scene in the boat is surely a bit like a Zen koan: it's a struggle for the mind to make any sense of it. Understanding our past trauma is a bit the same: what to do with it, and how to break through enough from insidious aftereffects to get a new perspective. Part of night sea journeying is about arriving at an authentic understanding, and becoming the person we are meant to be, rather than finding safety in past ways of coping, perhaps through compliance and falsity, or just through habit. The necessary breakthrough is about seeing it all more clearly.

Jesus urges the disciples to open themselves to the abundance and fullness on offer, as represented by the given numbers twelve, seven, four, seven, which McGann explains are all "richly symbolic within their tradition. They speak of abundance, fullness, perfection."[4] Jesus asks direct questions as a way of leading the consciousness of the disciples in a direction of greater spiritual insight, and awareness about a new way of thinking. We can read that the disciples are stuck in a literal temporal mind set: the previous miraculous feeding of the crowd have not shifted their belief system. There is also a feeling of conflict in the account exemplified in the warning: "Watch out—beware of the yeast of the Pharisees and the yeast of Herod." Destructive habits and rigid thought patterns,

3. Mark 8:14–21.

4. McGann, *Journeying Self*, 99.

even when they lessen, are insidious, as they can return again and again to take over our thinking—like the yeast in the dough permeating everywhere and expanding. None of this is surprising as our very neural pathways have been affected by our experiences, so new responses and reactions have to be painstakingly learned. Indeed, it is not until the disciples have been on their own night sea journeying, following the arrest of Jesus and the crucifixion, through Holy Saturday to the resurrection and beyond to Pentecost, when they will then fully understand the deeper spiritual dimension opened up by Jesus, and be true to themselves.

## THE HEALING OF THE BLIND MAN ON THE OTHER SIDE

This third sea voyage takes Jesus and the disciples over to Bethsaida, the place where distorted vision is treated: a blind man is brought for healing, mirroring the blindness and the fuzzy vision of the disciples, who still cannot get what Jesus is really talking about.[5] One interesting aspect of this healing of the blind man is that unlike all other healings in the Gospel it is not instantaneous, but requires Jesus' touching of the man's eyes twice. Recovery of sight, and it could be said in-sight, only happens gradually in this account. Jesus leads the man out of the village away from where he is known by his past, and by his infirmity

The first intimate touching, where Jesus places saliva on the man's eyes, leads to the man looking up, and seeing people as blurred objects like trees walking. With Jesus touching the man's eyes a second time, the man looks intently, and his sight is restored. By warning the man not to return to the village, Jesus is suggesting taking on a new perspective and a larger horizon. This account also helps us understand our own blurred vision: perhaps for a moment we can see beyond our usual comprehension, we take in a new experience, but then once again, a bit like the disciples, our vision becomes distorted and gradually shifts back to the status

5. Myers, *Binding*, 240.

quo. The something new that needs to happen for the survivor is a deeper mental and spiritual shift, which involves coming to grips with all sorts of emotions, including anger and ambivalence, and allowing these to surface, and to be put into words as feelings, and so in time gradually integrated. Our vision can be obscured by the past trauma. If we, like the blind man, can get ourselves outside the metaphorical village where our familiar thinking is limited, then we can raise our eyes to new horizons.

Evie

> I feel I got very trapped in my mind for many years—a bit like being in a cul de sac—interestingly I grew up in one—the house at the top where there never seemed a way out. I just kept repeating situations where I wasn't really being me, and just couldn't understand what was going wrong every time. I seemed to do it automatically, or unconsciously.
>
> One way of thinking I couldn't get out of was just plain embarrassing. I'd find myself longing for approval from older women, and then it would go badly wrong. One example was in spiritual direction. I'd met with this lovely spiritual director for a number of years, and that was all helpful and positive, and then she retired and suggested someone else. Initially I was fine, but then I began to feel more and more false with this [new] person. She was much more directive, even controlling, than the first person. I ended up feeling like a cardboard cutout, and was just saying things so that she would like me more, or thinking of what I could say that was what she wanted to hear. At one point I said I wanted to study theology more as I knew she was interested in that, and that got her very enthusiastic and smiling. Finally, I kind of realized what I was doing and stopped seeing her, but she was terribly upset, implying I hadn't been grateful enough for what she offered. The last meeting was ghastly . . . She said she thought something evil had entered the room, that I was leaving her on her own, and she told me to go to the church near where she lived, and seek forgiveness for stopping the sessions. I did what she wanted, but I'd left

my car in her drive, so I had to wait ages in case she was looking out of the window to see if I'd repented for long enough! Ridiculous, I should have just left, and I badly wanted to, but I felt too guilty.

The thing was I had been unfair to her too, as I'd sort of led her on, and then I rejected her . . . It was after that I thought I must try and understand more why this happens. But it was hard, almost as if I couldn't work it out. To her credit I think she sort of understood something about what was going on, as she wrote to apologize for the way she'd handled our meeting, and then she said if you ever look for a spiritual director again, I suggest you choose a man . . . I had also realized it was to do with my mother, and I was somehow repeating my relationship with all these other women, and perhaps hoping for a better outcome or a better mother! Or alternatively treating them in a way I wished I'd been able to with my mother: so, I apologized to her too.

Some years after both my parents had died, and incidentally, after the business with the spiritual director, I was contacted out of the blue by a third cousin—turned out to be my closest relative left on my mother's side. We corresponded by email as he lived abroad, and I asked him if he knew anything about my mother's background and history as she had always refused to say anything. For example, I knew nothing about my grandparents . . . It turned out that he was a keen family history buff, which is how he had tracked me down, and he was able to reveal a family secret that my grandmother had killed herself, leaving my mother to be brought up by her strict grandmother from a young age. My mother's brother had also died in a childhood accident, and my mother's father also died young. She had had a terrible time growing up. My immediate reaction was relief: what had happened, or rather hadn't happened between us, wasn't all my fault. No matter what, it would have been impossible for me to make all of *her* trauma better. I could also, and that took a lot of time, begin to feel some compassion for her; she didn't really know how to love or what family life could be like. The pressure must have contributed to all her illnesses, some of which I realized were to do with mental health. I got a whole new perspective realising that trauma had been passed on from generation to generation, and I felt some sort of heavy weight fall from me. It also made me determined to try to halt the damage for the next generation by trying to understand and sort it out inside me, rather than repeating too much of it.

Despite knowing all that and understanding the context better, some of the old ways of responding to events just wouldn't shift. The worst was catastrophic thinking, every time something happened, usually around one of my family not feeling well, or even the family pets, I had this sort of internal collapse. Even if one of the children just had a cold it felt like the end of the world, and then I had to work hard to control what I was feeling inside, or seek reassurance from someone. I remember once speaking to the school secretary to explain that my son still had a temperature, and she said "there's a lot of it about" and I immediately felt better, but it was all so tedious and, in the end, unnecessary, and very exhausting. . . . You see, no one had ever been able to tell me that things would be all right; partly because neither of my parents thought that themselves. Everyone was anxious.

It was much later in my life that I got a deeper understanding about my mind-body reactions. The big panic attacks had more or less stopped, but vestiges remained when anything dreadful happened—usually involving health issues. Some years back now I was very frightened about a medical test I had to have. In fact, I could scarcely breathe on the morning of the appointment, I was so terrified, asking God to help me be strong. I was getting dressed and listening to some music on the radio, when a voice from the radio said "be not afeared, be not afeared." It was a man's voice, quite calm, and spoke twice. I initially thought it was part of the music, which by the way was Edvard Grieg, "Wedding Day at Troldhaugen," so I went to try and find it on my phone, but there was no speaking—it was a piano piece. Sometime later, and by the way, the test was fine, I asked my then Jungian therapist whether he thought that God had spoken to me—I was worried I was going mad and hearing voices—and he said he thought it was highly likely it was God. After that I began to get a deeper sense of a spiritual dimension that underlay the old trauma response patterns, and my faith deepened. I didn't feel alone.

## GOD IN MY SOUL IS A CHILD—HOW TO FIND THE AUTHENTIC ME

In Mark's Gospel there is a central symbol found between the two stories of healing blind people: between the account at Bethsaida immediately after the sea voyage, and the account two chapters later of the healing of blind Bartimaeus (Mark 10:46). This central symbol is of a child, who is placed by Jesus in the middle of the group of disciples right in the midst of the blindness and darkness of the disciples' incomprehension. So how can this symbol of a child welcomed by Jesus help the adult survivor of a traumatic childhood?

Carl Jung, in his own experience of night sea journeying wrote, as quoted at the start of this book, how one of the insights he reached was that his soul was a child, and that God in his soul was as a child. What did Jung mean by this? Jung wanted to regain his soul and overcome spiritual alienation. To do this he needed to go down into the depths of his psyche to enable a rebirth of the image of God in his soul, that could become integrated.

This is part of what Jung called individuation, which he held to be a universal psychological development. For Jung, the symbol of the child was less to do with the "real" child who had been stunted by events, but rather a way of describing the life force and God. This is the divine child who is also Christ, the Self (with a capital "S") and God. This is the eternally springing youthfulness from which everything living comes. Jung writes about how in every adult there lurks an eternal child, something that is always in the process of becoming, and is never completed—the part of us that wants to become whole.[6]

6. Cf. Gardner, *Only Mind*.

The incarnated child that each of us is in the world has this twin: the divine child. Soul recovery is about the process of bringing these two parts of our soul together again for healing. If we can integrate enough of the feelings that have been repressed, there is a restoration to a wholeness, which now contains and includes the integrated experiences of the trauma. If we can find a space to feel safe and secure enough then the rigid control of our thinking can be eased, and some of the early developmental failure can be repaired. Joe found this in the group therapy, in his friendship with Andy, and through learning about mindful breathing and the practice of yoga. Evie found this through years in psychotherapy, through daily meditation and prayer, and in spiritual direction, and through hearing the voice of God.

In his account of healing from childhood trauma, James Finley describes an epiphany that led to a deeper understanding that broke through his defenses. After the abusive experiences at the Abbey of Gethsemani, and nearly a decade of trying to find his way by grounding himself in contemplative prayer and running retreats, Finley had begun a doctoral program to become a clinical psychologist. Part of the training included a placement in an in-patient alcohol treatment unit, where many of the men on the unit were Vietnam veterans suffering from post-traumatic stress disorder.

New men admitted to the unit had to undergo an initiation rite, which forced them to confront their alcoholism in a powerful and potentially life-changing way. Deeply affected by the ritual, and then the support offered by the other men to the new person once they had admitted that alcohol was what they loved best in the world, Finley was able to analyze what had happened, and what was needed for change to take place. In the moment of awakening, there was a deep vulnerability where the true self of the person was revealed, and fears were confronted. This was a moment where like a child the person was guileless and open-faced, free of posturing and posing. Here was the authentic spirit of the soul. Despite being alone, the initiate was also welcomed and embraced by the other men who had been through a similar realization, where old ways of being and thinking crumbled away. Finley here is referring to a deeper spiritual way of understanding what it means to understand. It is this that Jesus was trying to explain to the disciples in the boat on the sea voyage. This is not knowing about in the sense of a set of ideas, it's a deeper, different form of experiential knowing. Finley writes,

> In the vertical, depth dimension of the hidden foundations of inner liberation, to understand means to realize in some inexplicable way one's immersion in a fullness of Presence that cannot be explained.[7]

This experience is a fleeting taste of realized freedom offering a way through from the trauma, and from all the associated defensive symptoms. This is the presence of God.

> We, who have been blessed to have been drawn out onto the healing path, are discovering within ourselves that the polar opposite realms of traumatizing bitterness and tender sweetness are themselves permeated with the graced alchemy of a sustaining Presence that utterly transcends, even as it utterly permeates, the vicissitudes of all life might send our way.[8]

Religious experience, especially silent communion with God, can restore the person to a state that existed prior to the anxious development of a separate self, and prior to the fears and conflict that developed later. Fauteux sees this as deep reassurance, a rebuilding of the trust betrayed in infancy and childhood:

> The basic trust restored in the experience of God makes the person feel, as in the holding environment of infancy, that when frustrations and unanticipated problems arise, he can express the anxiety or previously forbidden feelings and God will not vanish.[9]

7. Finley, *Healing Path*, 117.
8. Finley, *Healing Path*, 121.
9. Fauteux, *Recovery of the Self*, 144.

As Evie and Joe found through their different journeying, the crucial thing is to open up, and acknowledge enough of the conflicts and fears that first caused the defensive development of the false self. There needs to be enough safety and security to access, contain and calm the trauma that is still registered somewhere in our bodies and minds. Authenticity is about finding a way of being and living that includes such experiences of the depths. Shelly Rambo calls this ability to include the depths as "transformation" and "redemption in the abyss of hell."[10] The trauma is present, it's what remains after the original suffering, but there can be a practice of witnessing to the trauma—again, physically, emotionally, and spiritually—that can give a sense of life arising, while acknowledging what remains.

As we become familiar with new ways of opening up and understanding the trauma and all the associated feelings, then concomitantly spiritual strengths arise. When feelings that have been locked up inside the wounded child are uncovered and released then something else comes with it. Emotions carry within them their own dynamic spiritual quality. For example, a spiritual strength of energy arises from getting to grips with anger and acknowledging our mixed feelings, our ambivalence. When anger is repressed it can become something monstrous as in dreams like Joe's of cruel tyrants, violent Nazis, and biting animals. Or it can become a frightening eruption from the unconscious as it is released in an apparently unconnected context. If our anger at what happened to us can be brought safely into the light, then the heat of anger can become a doorway into strength and constructive action. Our sadness can be a doorway into compassion, and fear can become a doorway into vulnerability.

Being in touch with emotions allows the hidden true self to begin to emerge, and this includes the numinous, soulful, and sacred. Part of soul recovery includes finding again something ineffable, the part of us that is forever, no matter what, a child of light. The inner child is still the damaged child who has suffered, but is also the inner child who holds sacred potential, the vital spark of

10. Rambo, *Spirit and Trauma*, 214.

one's own aliveness: you can still have life and have it abundantly despite what happened in the past.

# PART 3

# BACK ON THE LAND

# 8

# Where Sea, Land, and Sky Meet

Oh Lord our God . . . steer the ship of our life to yourself, the quiet harbour of all storm-stressed souls. Show us the course which we are to take.[1]

I lie on the seashore, the sparkling flood blue-shimmering in my dreamy eyes; light breezes flutter in the distance; the thud of the waves, charging and breaking over in foam, beats thrillingly and drowsily upon the shore—or upon the ear? . . . Nearer and nearer, friendlier, like a homecoming, sounds the thud of the waves; now, like a thundering pulse, they beat in my head, now they beat over my soul, wrapping it round, consuming it, while at the same time my soul floats out of me as a blue waste of waters. Outside and inside are one . . . The world expires in the soul and the soul dissolves in the world . . . Blue shimmers the infinite sea, where the jelly-fish dreams of that primeval existence to which our thoughts still filter down through aeons of memory. For every experience entails a change and a guarantee of life's unity. At that moment when they are no longer blended together, when the experient lifts his head, still blind and

1. Basil the Great, cited in Chiffolo, ed., *At Prayer*, 99.

> dripping, from immersion in the stream of experience, from flowing away with the thing experienced; when man, amazed and estranged, detaches the change from himself and holds it before him as something alien . . . and at that moment consciousness is born.[2]

Carl Jung in his work *Symbols of Transformation* quotes this extract from the work of the philosopher Karl Joel to illustrate rebirth into consciousness—the moment of breaking free from immersion in the stream of experience into an awareness of who we are, and how we have changed. The change that Jung discovered, from his journey away from outer things and into the depths, was that beyond the sadness and trauma lay a deeper reality where the soul is a living and independent being. First of all, he had to become aware of the loss of the soul, understanding that if he did not find his soul, "the horror of emptiness will overcome him." Then journeying into the depths, learning "that my soul finally lies behind everything, and if I cross the world, I am ultimately doing this to find my soul."[3]

So, here's the thing—change does and will happen, and over time it becomes easier to look back and feel, "that was then and this is now." Taking on the task of confronting the past involves the struggles and dark times of night sea journeying, and then periods when everything feels better and you're back on dry land. The sun shines. Then often the old feelings re-emerge, for the process is an ongoing spiral. It might feel as if one is back at the beginning of the journey again, but each time the experience is different and often increasingly easier to manage.

In this chapter we look first at the better times, the times of rebirth when it is possible to rediscover some spontaneity. Secondly, the idea of balancing the opposites is explored: the good times and the not so good; the love and the hate; the joy and despair. Then Jesus greeting the disciples on the seashore in the last chapter

2. Karl Joel quoted in Jung, *Symbols of Transformation*, para. 500.

3. Jung, *Red Book*, 231, 232.

of John's Gospel is used to discuss the idea of the transcendent function.

## COMING ASHORE: THE BLESSED GREENNESS OF THE LAND

Now the green blade riseth, from the buried grain,
Wheat that in the dark earth many days has lain;
Love lives again, that with the dead has been:
Love is come again, like wheat that springeth green.[4]

The *benedicta viriditas*, "blessed greenness," is taken from the writings of the twelfth-century Benedictine Abbess Hildegard von Bingen, and is about the greening power of God, and by extension the intrinsic power of human beings to grow and heal. She wrote "Hymn to the Holy Ghost," which begins: "From you the clouds rain down, the heavens move, the stones have their moisture, the waters give forth streams, and the earth sweats out greenness."[5]

The idea of greenness is one of Hildegard von Bingen's guiding images. She uses it as an expression of divinity, and the creative power of life that is mysteriously inherent in all life forms: plants, flowers, trees, animals, and in all the beautiful things of the world. The word *viriditas* is possibly derived from two Latin words: green and truth, and as well as its literal definition as in greenness and growth, there is also a metaphorical meaning as in freshness and vitality. Greenness is also present in the potential for all human beings to grow and to heal. The soul, as the life force in the body, is green, and spiritually this greening power lies at the heart of salvation; it is the force toward healing and wholeness and is the Word of God.

Remember that as Noah looked out over the endless sea from his ark, finally he saw the white dove return with the iconic olive branch: a sprig with green leaves, a symbol for peace, showing the

4. See Crum, "Love Is Come Again."
5. Jung, *Psychology and Religion*, para. 151.

end of the destruction of the flood, the withdrawal of the water, and a sign of hope and renewal. The olive branch can also be seen as a source of food, representing the dove's and every living creature's yearning for independence, and that life will thrive again.

> My beloved speaks and says to me: "Arise, my love, my fair one, and come away; for now the winter is past, the rain is over and gone. The flowers appear on the earth; and the time for singing has come, and the voice of the turtle dove is heard in our land. The fig tree puts forth its figs, and the vines are in blossom; they give forth fragrance."[6]

Jung is also attracted to the blessed greenness, as a psychospiritual state

> of someone who, in his wanderings among the mazes of his psychic transformation, comes upon a secret happiness which reconciles him to his apparent loneliness. In communing with himself he finds not deadly boredom and melancholy but an inner partner, more than that, a relationship that seems like the happiness of a secret love, or like a hidden springtime, when the green seed sprouts from the barren earth, holding of the promise of future harvests . . . the secret immanence of the divine spirit of life in all things. . . . Therefore this . . . might be called the Soul of the World.[7]

There is then a reconciliation between what has been and how one is. In this there can be movement of soul recovery and some healing of brokenness, where our healing is part of our purpose and leads to life's meaning. The trauma is brought further into the light of the sun, and in the soil of the struggle that has taken place through night sea journeying new growth becomes possible.

> Evie
>
> I don't take being on dry land for granted. I see it as a metaphor for having my feet firmly planted, and trying

6. Song of Solomon 2:10–13a.
7. Jung, *Mysterium*, para. 623.

to stay grounded, and as much as possible in the present moment rather than being drawn back to the past or past ways of responding. Once in a shop I bought a badge saying "It's never too late to have a happy childhood," and I hope that's true. Perhaps it's rather the chance to have moments of happiness—like a small child free to express themselves as they will.

"The price of freedom is eternal vigilance"—that's a saying attributed to Thomas Jefferson and I think it's been my way of life—or rather hypervigilance is the price of freedom, so you are always one step ahead of the next disaster. The irony is that I've found that what that means is you are never free. Now I see being free as when I'm not vigilant, when I'm absorbed or able to be spontaneous, and relax into what I'm doing, or who I am with. It happens if I'm busy at work, or caught up in a book, but it's best being outside.

Some time back, when I was in a particularly bad place emotionally, I found the only way to cope was just to walk, and walk, and walk some more. We're lucky enough to live in a small town where there's green countryside nearby, and that's where I often went, not with the children, nor with my husband, or a friend. Just me walking. I found that walking in town increased my anxiety during this time, but the minute I got near the town park, I felt I could breathe properly again. So, I avoided shops and streets, and aimed for fields. Very near me there's a meadow alongside the river where people walk their dogs, but I see it as a happy place as everyone is playing: dogs chasing balls, children on the swings and slide, and there's space, a lot of space. There's something about the soothing colour of the green grass and the big trees swaying in the wind, and the sky above, even if it's a grey sky—it's space. They say "action alleviates anxiety" and it's true. If I walk for long enough, my feet feeling the earth, then I can stop thinking, and when that happens it's so wonderful.

If, as explored in earlier chapters, trauma inhibits spontaneity and aliveness, then greening offers a chance for this to be partly remedied and encouraged. The color green as signifying the divine spirit of life in all things, became a central metaphor for Barbara, a woman in therapy with Donald Kalsched. Following a traumatic childhood with a mentally unstable mother and an emotionally distant father, she remembered being beside herself with fear when her mother acted out manically, often actually tearing the house apart. She hardened herself on the outside, trying to be good, while removing a part of herself emotionally on the inside. She described this as going to a cold, remote place.

As an adult, Barbara dreamt that she was on a cold, dying planet, invited to rescue any surviving creatures, and bring them back to Earth. The other being on the planet was one known as the emissary, which she couldn't see but could hear. At the end of the dream Barbara saw that the emissary was a green monster with a tentacle that wrapped itself around her and around the bundle of repulsive rescued animals that she was carrying. Barbara deduced that in the dream she both suffered the monster, but also loved him fiercely; somehow the green monster was a part of her that needed to be brought to Earth and to dry land.

In the process of her night sea journeying, new understanding emerged when Barbara learned that at sixteen months, she had been separated from her mother for six weeks, suffering a serious rupture in her early attachment. This set a pattern that was repeated in subsequent relationships and situations, and that left her with a deep sense of insecurity and an abiding threat of loss of love. Towards the end of her analysis with Kalsched, Barbara dreamt: "Green tendrils of a plant were waving in the breeze, with an accompanying voice-over that said: 'I am the true vine.'" While a simple image, it was clear that it was a further and meaningful development of the green monster dream. Kalsched immediately linked this to John's Gospel and read this section to Barbara:

> [Jesus said,] "I am the true vine and my father is the vinegrower. Every branch that bears fruit he prunes to make it bear more fruit . . . Just as the branch cannot bear fruit unless it abides in the vine, neither can you unless you abide in me. If you abide in me, ask for whatever you wish, and it will be done for you. My Father is glorified

> by this, that you bear much fruit. As the Father has loved me, so I have loved you; abide in my love. I have said these things to you so that my joy may be in you, and that your joy may be complete."[8]

Kalsched writes that for both him and Barbara, a deep spiritual truth flooded into the space, like a blessing,

> though neither of us could grasp its full meaning . . . In that moment, the wisdom of the psyche came into full view. It was as though the *benedicta viriditas*—the blessed greenness—had settled over us both, blessing us, and filling the "third" space between us with a beauty and a mystery whose meaning could only be sensed and felt, not fully known.[9]

## BALANCING THE PSYCHE: THE CROSSING AND RECROSSING OF THE SEA OF GALILEE

Jesus, in Mark's Gospel, pays equal attention to both sides of the lake; a great deal of time is spent crossing back and forth between the two sides of the water. One way of looking at this from a Jungian perspective is of Christ seen here as reconciling the two sides: the opposites. From a psychological view, when the psyche is balanced energy is free to flow, and the soul moves outward in creativity. This holding the tension and reconciling of opposites is at the heart of Mark's Gospel, at the center of spirituality, and also at the center of the balanced psyche.

Carl Jung understood that one can only get a sense of the whole, and achieve some sort of balance, by nurturing one's opposite. This is the coincidence, in the sense of the co-existence, of the opposites. Giving space to the opposing emotions and differing parts of the psyche is extremely difficult, as is trying to find a way to try to unite them—so much so that the phrase of "holding the tension of the opposites" sums up the psychological and spiritual

8. John 15:1–11.
9. Kalsched, *Trauma and the Soul*, 238–39.

effort involved. This tension Jung thought could become resolved through compromise, or finding a way just through living. Thomas Merton in his study of the same idea saw it as part of what it means to be creative. As we struggle to cope with the different parts of our psyche, so we find a third way that has been called the transcendent function, something that is more than the two opposites and a creative new spiritual energy.

Both Merton and Jung drew on the writings of Nicholas of Cusa, who saw the coincidence of opposites as a methodology for knowing God, a method where contradiction between opposites is acknowledged, reconciled, and surpassed. The impossibility is transcended to where God is beyond all difference, and so the soul is transformed. Cusa writes:

> When I am at the door of the coincidence of opposites, guarded by the angel stationed at the entrance of paradise, I begin to see you, O Lord. For you are where speaking, seeing, hearing, tasting, touching, reasoning, knowing and understanding are the same and where seeing coincides with being seen, hearing with being heard, tasting with being tasted, touching with being touched, speaking with hearing, and creating with speaking.[10]

Holding the tension of the opposites also lies at the heart of soul recovery from a traumatizing childhood. If we can hold the apparent contradictions and opposite experiences, and recognize and no longer mask our self-contradictions, then there can be some sort of balance and equilibrium that allows us to continue to creatively live and develop. One such contradiction is holding the reality of what has happened alongside respecting (rather than castigating) ourselves for the ways in which our psyches have found to cope with this. The psychoanalyst Margaret Arden writes of this:

> When a person comes to understand the core of his or her childhood experience, all the anger, all the rejection of life, turns out to have been for one purpose—to

10. Bond, ed., *Nicholas of Cusa*, 252–53.

> preserve, at whatever cost, the child who is capable of love.[11]

An awareness of these different states of mind is a huge achievement, one that will ultimately lead to self-acceptance and so to soul recovery. Another contradictory experience is that despite unraveling, experiencing, and, understanding the psychic truth of what happened, it all still remains. Both Evie and Joe had thought at different times that there could be a solution that would somehow make everything ideal, but they found the reality was more complex.

> Joe
>
> Whilst the group therapy and talking with Matt and the others certainly helped as it got me off the sofa and into trying to change my life, in the end the talking stuff wasn't really me. The real breakthrough, as I've said before, was finding yoga and getting to know my body again in a kind and positive way, and learning and talking with Andy. I've worked out that yoga began to heal me because so much of the trauma was held in my body, and it was listening to my body and feeling grounded that really helped. When I first began the yoga practice and classes, I was very excited as I thought that if I worked enough physically, then I could somehow wipe out the whole "failure to thrive" label . . . I would become "success at growing" instead! I wanted to make a great success of it to forget. . . . What I know now is that opening up and unravelling the past is no longer about reaching any goal, but rather about what one yoga teacher calls "a gradual unfolding, an effortless blossoming."[12]
>
> While I can breathe out the old stories, they will always be there, but now it's a positive reason to make changes not just for myself, but for other people too. What I found was that the me doing yoga in the present became more important than the depressed me in the past, and that I could gradually see that that was then and

11. Arden, *Midwifery*, 4–5.
12. Sabatini, *Breath*, 13.

this is now. Before just seeing myself as deprived made me one-sided, but it's balanced out by who I am now. Of course, a lot of yoga is about being balanced too. You do postures on one side, and then on the other, and for some things you time your breath: inhale and then followed by exhale; holding the full breath after you've inhaled, and then the opposite holding the breath that has been emptied at the bottom of the exhale. Part of the breathing was to breathe really deeply into my whole body and feel nourished by that, then breathing out to let go of something, a release from old wounds. The breathing out was letting go of the old stories. I found the more I could subtract and give up the stories stored in my body, the more I could find happiness. So, the whole thing began to feel more about opening, softening, and strengthening. . . . I was spending a lot of time balancing my mind and body.

After training as a yoga teacher, I led classes and also did individual work. Eventually I also taught on the same training course that I had done. I also trained as a breath coach and so now, alongside the yoga, that's what I do for a living—imagine earning money for breathing! One of the later yoga training courses I did was abroad, and with this amazing guy Eoin Finn, who would say "turn your stressings into blessings," and "you deserve love and you deserve happiness, tune into the joy you were meant to feel as a child," and he talks about contacting "the wise guide inside."[13] And yes, I can have some of that as well as knowing how sad and low I was at times, and sometimes still get. It's both/and, not either/or. The thing about the yoga and the mindful breathing is it's actually deeply spiritual, without being formally religious. I do now believe that God or a divine spirit was looking out for me, but half the time I couldn't, or was it rather that, I wouldn't listen. And then there was that message in the hospital from Jesus when I was waiting for the psychiatrist, which now looking back I think was the start of all the changes. I don't think going to church would have suited me, because there's too many words, and there's all

13. Finn, "Blissology Project Metta."

that mixed messaging about the body and being gay too. My church is on the yoga mat.

One of the newer practices I've been learning about and using over the last few years is called yoga Nidra, it's a different form of relaxation and breath awareness: what you do is explore the opposites in terms of body sensation . . . Well, you are guided on a body scan, and then what's happening emotionally and what your beliefs about yourself are . . . You go for what's negative, but then you identify an extreme opposite of that feeling. You go back and forth but it's helped by the guidance about breathing. Basically, it loosens up the negative and helps you to accept these opposites, and so tolerate and be aware of what happens in your life. Part of the guided practice is then you are encouraged to find awareness that embraces these opposites, and that can help establish a third realistic thought between the two opposites.

## STANDING ON THE BEACH—THE IDEA OF THE TRANSCENDENT FUNCTION

Lead me to the rock that is higher than I, for you have been my refuge.[14]

Joe's insights can be seen to link with the work that Carl Jung did when he was undertaking his own night sea journeying. At that time, Jung began to formulate his thinking on what he called the transcendent function, where this tension of bearing opposite experiences and feelings can be held by a third force greater than the two that differ from one another, and which can often be symbolized in a way that contains and holds the opposites enough to unify and transcend them. For Jung, God was one such symbol, which lay outside the conscious ego and was the source of all creativity. God is more than oneself yet within oneself, another contradiction, but one that can give a breakthrough from a closed state of mind into openness. God acts as a third force and serves as a way

14. Psalm 61:2b.

of containing and superseding what appears impossible. Thomas Merton writes about trying to hold opposites and disparate aspects of ourselves, and transcend them in Christ. He realized that there was meaning in trying to hold difference. He wrote: "The real order of the cosmos is an apparent disorder, the 'conflict' of opposites which is in fact a stable and dynamic harmony."[15]

Coming ashore and to a safe harbor is about journeying toward acceptance, with all the contradictory feelings involved; and it takes a struggle to remain in balance when there are so many mixed feelings involved. Here is the possibility of a feeling of integration, but one achieved despite, or because of, differences. The transcendent function then is one of the ways that the psyche seeks connection between disparate and opposite experiences so as to continually evolve and grow. It can never be a constant state of mind, but, perhaps, from time to time we can experience transcendent moments helped by the something more than ourselves. Even the slightest insight that there is a divine inner other that can guide human consciousness is transformational. It changes the person who goes through such an illuminative and revelatory process, leaving them with a different type of understanding of true reality from people who have not had such an experience.

In John's Gospel, the account of the risen Christ meeting some of the disciples on the seashore shows Christ as the transcendent function, holding and containing all the contradictions of recent events, and from them bringing new meaning and developments. In the account, Peter as leader has decided after the trauma of Jesus' death to return to his work as a fisherman. In the light of all the contradictions about what has happened, and presumably feeling the impossibility of coping with and making sense of recent events, Peter returns in the dark to the familiar work of fishing, and takes some of the others with him. While aware that Jesus was alive again, the group had no idea what to do with that reality: going back to work was one solution. The immediate contradiction is that while returning to the old way of being seems the obvious solution after a crisis, it will no longer do: "they caught nothing."

15. Merton, "Herakleitos the Obscure," 263.

At daybreak the voice of an apparent stranger standing on the seashore then reveals to them what has been hidden. Those in the fishing boat need to turn their attention to the other side: "Cast your net to the right side of the boat." In other words, they need to work from the opposite side. A new perspective has to emerge.

When they meet on the shore after catching many fish, the disciples now have a contribution to make, and Christ invites them to bring some of what they have caught and adds what is his. "Jesus said to them, 'Come and have breakfast.'"[16] As Diarmuid McGann notes, what the disciples have taken from the water becomes their nourishment, but only after Jesus has "taken it and blessed it and given it to them."[17] The fruits from the sea have been transformed by the divine spirit, and it is the two contributions that then make the meal.

Other contradictions also have to be contained and transcended. One of these is Peter's betrayal of Jesus on the night of Jesus' arrest, in apparent contradiction with Peter's professed love and discipleship. How can this be held, understood, and transcended? The ensuing dialogue between Jesus and Peter acknowledges Peter's feelings of fear and persecution when he was questioned three times about his association with Jesus. Each time he had answered by denying knowing, respecting, and loving Jesus. The mixed feelings and what happened are not forgotten, but redeemed, and then transcended by the re-commissioning of Peter to be the leader he was called to be. It has been suggested that in the first questioning—"Jesus said to Simon Peter, 'Simon, son of John, do you love me more than these?'"[18]—that Jesus is asking, "Do you love me more than (you love) these things (your fishing nets and equipment)?"—that is, "Are you going back to your former trade or will you continue to follow me?"[19] In the context of night sea journeying, once back on the shore we are invited to think about where our allegiance lies. The question is whether we are still deeply attached

16. John 21:1–23.

17. McGann, *Journeying within Transcendence*, 194.

18. John 21:15

19. Greenlee, "More than These?," 20.

to our old way of being, including the defenses that have helped us to survive adequately, or, whether we can take on a different way of being. This is the essence of soul recovery. Restoration signals a new beginning, but the past is not forgotten.

Jesus Christ welcomes us in the liminal place where land and sky, earth and heaven meet. Christ waits and welcomes us onto the seashore, where there can be a form of holding different experiences and integrating them. After night sea journeying the trauma is no longer stuck or frozen underneath the water of life. The experience gives a grounding and belief in resilience, for having survived what at the time felt annihilating. The trauma that took place in childhood carries significance about what it means to be human. Engaging with the night sea journeying, and finding there the presence of something more than ourselves, certainly does not mean that suffering is sent by God to try people. That would be morally unacceptable. But it can be the case that adverse experiences mean that people do sometimes learn more about themselves, and may even be moved to a deeper awareness, spiritually and psychologically.

The resources for soul recovery are within us as inner resources, and outside us in terms of community and relationships. Spiritual recovery from trauma needs divine inspiration to reinvigorate our soul, our true self. Carl Jung in his experiments with night sea journeying gained the insight that "the other whom we do not know," which he called "The Self, "is in each of us and can speak to us in our dreams: "When, therefore, we find ourselves in a difficult situation to which there is no solution, he can sometimes kindle a light that radically alters our attitude."[20] This spiritual presence is, Jung explains, the long-expected friend of our soul—"the immortal one," who, set free, can then lead us into what Jung describes as "that greater life"—an integrated life.[21] In Mark's Gospel, as Jesus travels back and forth across the Sea of Galilee he is holding, connecting, integrating, and transcending the opposites: a metaphor for soul recovery.

20. Kalsched, *Trauma and the Soul*, 128.

21. Jung, *Archetypes*, para. 217.

# 9

# Beyond the Night

Christianity discerns that beyond the night
The dawn already glows
The hope that does not fail is carried in the heart
Christ goes with us![1]

IN THIS FINAL CHAPTER, two ideas are explored, and both are about acceptance. The first is about accepting that the past remains as somewhere that we are at times inevitably drawn back to; the second is about developing self-acceptance. With both types of acceptance, which are of course deeply interconnected, there comes hope.

Mark's Gospel is pervaded by evening and night darkness, perhaps to emphasize what Jesus has to engage with, and ultimately overcome. The first two sea journeys described in this book take place in the dark; quite probably the third too as it seems to be happening at the end of the day. In the Gospel, as darkness becomes increasingly oppressive, so inevitably the light of the morning is increasingly desired. The evening gospel is finally followed by the dawn epiphany, with the prospect of hope and renewal. In night sea journeying the dark is punctuated with moments of insights—epiphanies—and glimpses of a dawn breaking through as healing

1. Romero, *Violence of Love*, 165.

begins to take place. Yet, it is accepted that another evening will follow the bright day.

James Finley writes how hard it was to free himself from what he calls "my longstanding survival strategy of feeling safe." This included knowing how to let others think he was there talking with them, when in reality, and without them knowing, "I had already retreated into the dissociative cave where no one but God could find me." He calls this one of the emotionally distancing habits from which he was sincerely trying to break free from, over decades. It was partly because of his work in psychotherapy and spiritual direction that Finley came to understand how hard it is to see and accept how powerless we are to break free from these wounded and wounding patterns. It is only by appreciating this that we can begin to understand how any path to healing circles back again and again in order to, as Finley sees it,

> cultivate within ourselves a more merciful understanding of ourselves as we learn to see, love, and respect the still-confused and wounded aspects of ourselves. . . . We are now attempting to bear witness to the sweet secret of experiential salvation in which the torn and ragged edges of our wounded and wayward hearts are experienced as . . . the opening through which the gentle light of God's merciful love shines into our lives.[2]

## ACCEPTANCE THAT THERE IS NO "AFTER" IN TRAUMA

Harry Guntrip, a religious minister who became a psychoanalyst, was severely traumatized as a three-year-old by the death of his baby brother. Guntrip suffered amnesia, until after two long periods of analysis that, as he describes it, had "softened the repression," he had a breakthrough at the age of seventy. For all those years the trauma, he writes, "remained alive in me, to be triggered off unrecognized by widely spaced analogous events." He experienced what

2. Finley, *Healing Path*, 160–62.

he described as "mysterious exhaustion illnesses," and feelings of "alienation and unreality." Yet what Guntrip understood from his personal experiences was that he had no option other than to pursue what he called "the long quest" to make sense of the past, and how it affected him in the present. His night sea journeying turned into "a vocation through which I might help others." Guntrip remembers how his first analyst, Ronald Fairbairn, stated:

> The basic pattern of personality once fixed in early childhood, can't be altered. Emotion can be drained out of the old patterns by new experience, but water can always flow again in the old dried up water courses.[3]

Trauma can never be eradicated. No one can have a different history, but we can reach a place where somehow it does not always matter quite so much to us anymore. If we can learn to trust again through a healing relationship with another, then soul recovery begins. It is a process of interaction, where there is a working together towards free spontaneous growth, and both change during the experience. Guntrip describes this in therapy as

> the provision of a reliable and understanding human relationship of a kind that makes contact with the deeply repressed traumatized child in a way that enables one to become steadily more able to live, in the security of a new real relationship, with the traumatic legacy of the earliest formative years, as it seeps through or erupts into consciousness.[4]

A healing relationship may be through a formal process such as psychotherapy or spiritual direction, but it can also happen in personal relationship and experiences of God—that is the divine who is more than ourselves. This then becomes a process of learning to trust ourselves again so we can tap into our private wisdom, and the natural healing of the mind, where painful truths that have been denied and repressed for years can now be tolerated. It includes respecting and acknowledging our defensive ways

3. Guntrip, *Personal Relations*, 351, 358, 351, 351, 352, 366, respectively.
4. Guntrip, *Personal Relations*, 366.

of behaving, but relying on them less as psychological crutches. Such a shift needs sufficient self-belief to cope with the depression that accompanies the painful past. It is again about holding the different feelings: taking what happened seriously, alongside a developing capacity to enjoy life realistically—a minimum of illusion alongside a dose of disillusionment. The breakthrough is accepting the unhappy realization that the experience of suffering all over again has been necessary for soul recovery, and that paradoxically the healing has come from the longings of the soul *itself* to be a life-giver. We are both healed and not healed, but with potential for increasing openness to the divinity that transcends all our circumstances.

The work of the theologian Shelly Rambo is immensely helpful here. She writes about living with the scars, referring to the wounds still found on the body of the resurrected Christ: "The resurrection narratives provide testimonies to life beyond trauma. . . . [It is] a theology of resurrection that addresses returning wounds." Rambo gives a trauma-informed analysis of Jesus' response to doubting Thomas: "Then he said to Thomas, 'Put your finger here and see my hands. Reach out your hand and put it in my side. Do not doubt but believe.'"[5] Resurrection is one with the crucifixion and acknowledgment of the wounds, but also new configurations of life on the other side of what happened. Rambo writes:

> The Jesus who returns cuts through fear and exposes his wounds . . . marking the impossibility of erasure. These are the wounds that when they reappear in the present, not only carry the past suffering lodged in the body but, also, as Jesus instructs the disciples, require a different way of seeing.[6]

> Joe

> After all the hard graft in the therapy group and then in Depressives Anonymous, and also when I was

5. John 20:27.

6. Rambo, *Resurrecting Wounds*, 11, 88.

beginning yoga—all that was a real effort and seemed to take forever . . . and then, after a few years, I noticed I was feeling better. Over the next couple of decades, I suppose I felt pretty pleased with myself—I had trained and travelled around doing yoga training courses, got my qualifications and set up a business. The yoga classes were popular and I felt I'd put the past firmly behind me. I was in a relationship with this wonderful guy and life seemed peachy. But then came COVID and everything stopped—suddenly I couldn't be busy any more, and then I caught COVID and felt really rough. I found myself back on the sofa just lying and sleeping. There was no way I could keep myself busy because I had no energy, also I had to be on my own as I didn't want my partner to catch COVID. So, I found myself back in depression—probably partly the virus, but also definitely alongside it old, old stuff—sadly I recognized it and thought—oh, that's what I used to feel, I thought I'd never have to feel this again—aaah. And then I got very frightened—suppose I couldn't get out of it?

I wasn't sure I wanted back on anti-depressants, but I did begin to realize that all that crap stuff had never really gone away—and then the huge realisation that no matter what I did, it was always going to be part of me. But I didn't want to lose everything I'd built up, and I certainly didn't want the trauma to define me—there's more to me now than that underfed, unloved, and miserable child stuck on the sofa watching TV all day. So, somehow, I got enough energy to begin to do some work online with a course about trauma, and then from that found someone doing spiritual direction work but from a trauma-informed position. It was hugely helpful, and one of the things that came through was how as a toddler I had had to keep myself alive, despite the collapse and just sitting on the sofa. It wasn't until Mum and Dad came along that I could begin to let them take over, and be a proper child—confident that I would get enough to eat and some love too. Then as a teenager, there was all the keep fit stuff. But when I got to adulthood and it seemed as if it was all up to me again, I went back to just lying around. So, once I came out of the depression then and found out what to do with my life, I was working harder and harder to keep myself in existence, and so to speak off the sofa—it was like I became afraid to stop being busy—as if I might stop existing again. So, I got to know how important being active was—even if ironically, I was also doing calm breathing and yoga workouts—but I couldn't just be, or rather relax into being me. And then COVID forced me back on the sofa and that was for weeks . . . no tell the truth, it was months.

One of the people I found online during this time was Thich Nhat Hanh and that proved really helpful, because he understood that you need to make a solid base within yourself by practicing breathing mindfully. He got that people are afraid—it's part of being human, but when the fear comes up it is fear that you've felt before, and you survived before, so the chances are you'll survive again. It's like being caught in a storm, but the storm then passes, and it's calm again. One of his great quotes is about how the lotus flower is a wonder, but a wonder that only exists because of the mud from which it grew—and the mud is also a wonder. You can touch the kingdom of God, he says, not only in the lotus, but also in the mud. We get an understanding by looking deeply into our suffering, and from that there is then a chance for happiness to blossom. Wonderful stuff! [7]

When I was feeling more myself again, we went to Sri Lanka for a holiday—I suppose I wanted to see where I had come from. It was beautiful—absolutely stunning, though they've had their political and violent troubles over there too. One of the places we visited was Polonnaruwa. My spiritual director, knowing I was going had told me about Thomas Merton's visit there, and whilst I didn't have the same experience when I saw the huge Buddhist statues, I too was filled with a sense of deep awe and gratitude about being alive, and the strange, mixed journey that I've been on in my life. Merton writes this:

> Looking at these figures I was suddenly, almost forcibly, jerked clean out of the habitual, half-tied vision of things, and an inner clearness, clarity, as if exploding

7. See Plum Village App, "No Mud No Lotus."

> from the rocks themselves, became evident and obvious . . . The thing about all this is that there is no puzzle, no problem, and really "no mystery." All problems are resolved and everything is clear, simply because what matters is clear. . . . Everything is emptiness and everything is compassion.[8]
>
> What Merton said made me realize then that this balance between suffering and joy, and doing and being, is central. If needs be I can be in the fear and accept what happened to me, but also now be the grown-up me with plans, and ideas, and enjoy being alive. I now have skills and methods of getting out of the depression as best as I can. What happened is like the ground out of which everything else has grown, and if I can hold onto that, then it's easier to get out of the low times again. At least that's my hope, and I really think now what I believe. Being alive is a miracle, but oh so very strange: so much beauty and so much suffering, and there's a deep spiritual reality beyond and within all this that somehow holds it together.

Joe's acceptance of what has happened resonates with this description from Oscar Wilde. Towards the end of his imprisonment in the early months of 1897, the poet and playwright wrote "De Profundis." This extract encapsulates his own journey:

> I saw then that the only thing for me was to accept everything. Since then—curious as it will no doubt sound—I have been happier. It was of course my soul in its ultimate essence that I had reached. In many ways I had been its enemy, but I found it waiting for me as a friend.
>
> Now I find hidden, somewhere away in my nature, something that tells me that nothing in the whole world is meaningless, and suffering least of all . . .
>
> It's the last thing left in me, and the best: the ultimate discovery at which I have arrived, the starting point for a fresh development. It has come to me right out of myself . . . It is the one thing that has in it the elements of life . . .

8. See Merton, *Other Side*, 323.

> The important thing . . . is not to be maimed, marred, and incomplete, is to absorb into my nature all that has been done to me, to make it part of me, to accept it . . .[9]

## SELF-ACCEPTANCE: "WHO DO I SAY THAT I AM?"

In the epilogue to his autobiography, Harry Williams writes how different the reality of his life is from the ideal version. Yet that if he were given the choice, it would be to be what he actually *is*, rather than the ideal. Although not achieving peace, Williams writes, he has caught glimpses of glory now and then. He adds:

> Nothing is for nothing. You always have to pay for what you get. Without pain there can be no birth; without death no resurrection. In that necessity the ideal and the actual are reconciled and seem to belong inescapably to each other.[10]

Similarly, from Carl Jung's night sea journeying it becomes clear that there is no personal growth without suffering, and that there can be no progress without personal growth. He discovered that his life was lived in two worlds—earth-rooted and spiritually centered, and both he saw as the natural state of realized humanity. He knew that he contained a clash of opposites, and strove to live and reconcile all this into some sort of wholeness—this is then the process he called individuation. At eighty-four he said of that long trek:

> The journey from cloud cuckoo land to reality lasted a long time. In my case Pilgrim's Progress consisted in my having to climb down a thousand ladders until I could reach out my hand to the little clod of earth that I am.[11]

9. Wilde, cited in Phillips, *Choice is Always Ours*, 122.
10. Williams, *Some Day I'll Find You*, 383.
11. Jung, *Letters 1*, 19n.

For Jung, a telling question of one's life is are we related to something infinite or not? For Jung the infinite is what truly matters, and only if we embody the awareness of ourselves as both finite and infinite, limited and eternal. In a letter to his friend Father Victor White, Jung wrote of the necessity of conscious suffering, and where doubt and insecurity are indispensable components of a complete life.

> Only those who can lose this life *really* can gain it. A "complete" life does not consist in a theoretical completeness, but in the fact that one accepts, without reservation, the particular fatal tissue in which one finds oneself embedded, and that one tries to make sense of it or to create a cosmos from the chaotic mess into which one is born. If one lives properly and completely, time and again one will be confronted with a situation of which one will say: "This is too much. I cannot bear it any more." Then the question must be answered: "Can one really not bear it?"[12]

Here is the heart of self-acceptance—the acceptance of "the fatal tissue" of where we find ourselves, and "the chaotic mess" into which one is born, both at the personal level and in the societal and collective level. Self-acceptance is the recognition that one survived this mess once, and indeed survived again and again when the experiences resurfaced. With self-acceptance, we can live without pretense and without concern that others are judging us negatively. Realigning with the soul—the life-giver—takes us beyond being a survivor, as we witness to what happened, and, to what one's life has become in the light of the suffering. This is about becoming fully human, accepting that one is human and so accepting the human condition.

Kalsched describes this as the tragic beauty of being alive, letting "the innocent (God-identified) part of us suffer experience in order to grow a soul . . ."[13] He sees this as the ultimate meaning of the cross, where trauma leads to the indwelling of the soul,

12. Jung, *Letters 2*, 171.

13. Kalsched, *Trauma and the Soul*, 241.

and where in our earth-bound suffering—the darkness slowly becomes changed and leads to en-*light*-en-ment through a divine redeeming presence that brings meaning, and sometimes joy and gratitude. With soul recovery there is a deeper dimension of this presence. The image of God embedded within the soul brings what another Jungian, Marie von Franz, called sparks of divine illumination. For her, God is "the innermost nucleus of the soul and at the same time the cosmic divine All-Spirit."[14] Rebecca Parker, as an adult survivor, writes of this spiritual revelation:

> I knew that in the end all there is, is mercy. The promise was true. Weeping may endure for the night, but joy comes in the morning. . . .
>
> Somehow my life is marked by this legacy of presence. And this is how I can speak of God: a presence gradually unfolded by life in its richness and tragedies, its devastating losses and its abundance; a power calling us into fullness of living; a passion for life, for good and ill; an unquenchable fire at the core of life, glimpsed in light and shadows.[15]

> Evie
>
> Oh, dear, it's taken me so very long first of all to accept the past, and all the traumas from my childhood, and even longer to recognize, and accept, all the defences that I put in place to protect myself over so many years. It's been a bit of a breakthrough to accept: that's how it was, and with all the body memory stuff that sometimes rushes up again to accept: that's how it is. For years I thought I could be healed in such a way that I could forget all about it—I would be completely cured, but the healing hasn't been like that. A lot of the past has faded, but sometimes the old emotions come rushing up again, but in a new context where I've been unexpectedly triggered, so I've had to find ways to be despite all that. I can't

14. Von Franz, *Dreams*, 12–13.

15. Brock and Parker, *Proverb of Ashes*, 215, 233.

rely on it not resurfacing, and I can't rely on other people to manage it for me.

In my first therapy the analyst I saw lent me her book called *The Courage to Be,* by Paul Tillich, and I carried that book around for ages, not so much reading it but rather taking inspiration from the title.[16] Clearly psychotherapy and spiritual direction greatly helped, but deepening my faith has shifted it all hugely—in one way my most honest relationship now is with God. I have no hesitation in turning to God, and to Christ to help me and to guide me. I like the idea that Jesus Christ sees all of me including my woundedness, so it feels that in some ways what happened has been redeemed by that acceptance. I now believe in radical, unconditional acceptance of *all of us* by the wounded and traumatized Jesus Christ, and the idea of healing within wounds: "by his wounds you are healed."[17] It's through the wounds that the light of Christ can appear.

Practicing a daily liturgy sounds old-fashioned, but there's something about reciting psalms, prayers, and readings that millions have said over the years: praising, thanking, asking, and pleading that holds me grounded. I like the routine; it definitely centers me, and it feels like an essential part now of each morning and evening. Somehow the day is held by the habit. Am I always present to God then? Well, no—but it gives me a chance to be. I do go to church, but it's not always a safe space for me, and I think most people I know there wouldn't really get much of the stuff I've spoken about—and I wouldn't want to discuss it with them anyway. I go for the Eucharist, which I think is central—where the wounded Christ welcomes me, another wounded soul, to his table. I said earlier that as a child I was never reassured, no one around me was able to say that things would be all right, mainly because they didn't believe that themselves, so when I read how Jesus had spoken to the mystic Julian of Norwich that, "All will be well, and all will be well, and

16. Tillich, *Courage to Be.*

17. 1 Peter 2:24.

> all manner of thing will be well," I felt I could take that as spoken to me too.[18]
>
> When Jesus asks the disciples if they want to stay or go, and Simon Peter replies "Lord, to whom can we go? You have the words of eternal life,"[19] a bit like what else is there, and that's where I am at present.
>
> There's still the past, but there's a better sense of who I am too in the present in the sense of being freer—more spontaneous and there's still more to discover. I feel I know myself pretty well now. It's ongoing—no finished product—but I get it, it's all about times of unravelling and then gathering up again.

To accept ourselves we need to be able to feel love for ourselves, and for those who had a traumatic childhood this is always difficult. Infancy is really the only time in our lives where we can each be loved for just being alive, loved for just being born and there. If all goes well, we feel beloved for being. If unconditional love didn't happen, or happen enough, or was interrupted by trauma, how do we find the way to love ourselves? Perhaps, just perhaps, it can come through an experience or belief in the something more than ourselves, whatever name we give to this. Marsha Linehan, psychologist, therapist, and author, offers one experience of how this suddenly and unexpectedly happened for her.

> I was sitting in that sitting room right outside the chapel . . . which I will never forget because I was sitting on the couch and I think I felt complete and total despair—and this nun walked by and she turned and looked and said "Is there anything I can do for you?" And I realized that no-one could help me. No-one. I said no thank you and she left and so I got up and went into the chapel and I was just looking at the cross above the altar and then out of the blue—out of the complete blue—suddenly everything became golden. And suddenly I felt something coming towards me. The crucifix started shimmering and the room was shimmering and I had this unbelievable

18. Julian of Norwich, *Revelations*, 55.

19. John 6:68.

> experience of God loving me. I jumped up and ran out and ran to my room and I was standing in my room and I said out loud "I love myself!" And the minute, the very minute the word *myself* came out of my mouth, I knew I had been completely transformed. Because up until that point I would never have said that. I would have said I love *you*. Because I had no sense of *myself*. I thought of myself as you. The minute the word myself came from my mouth, I knew—and I've always known ever since—that I would never cross that line again, into being crazy.[20]

## HOPE THAT DOES NOT FAIL IS CARRIED IN THE HEART CHRIST GOES WITH US.

From acceptance of what has happened to us, and from self-acceptance, can come hope. For Thomas Merton hope is founded on God's acceptance and love of *us*. Such hope confirms to us that divine mercy and goodness are more powerful than the darkness of the past trauma. For Merton, hope is about establishing "a right relationship between the past and the future, which can give spiritual solidity to the present."[21] Merton, as a traumatized child understood as an adult that authentic hope develops not by avoiding the darkness and apparent emptiness of life, nor by adopting a false optimism by suppression of what he calls tragic realities, but rather by entering the darkness of suffering and discovering meaning and life even there. This journey of entering into the darkness, which might look from the outside as both absurd and morbid, ultimately leads to the deeper reality of soul recovery. Merton understood that "perfect hope is achieved on the brink of despair, when, instead of falling over the edge, we find ourselves walking on air."[22]

20. Linehan, "Moment I Was Transformed."
21. Merton, *Search for Solitude*, 354.
22. Merton, *No Man Is an Island*, 182.

Why is this? For Merton it is as we connect with the traumatized Christ where, we find ourselves in

> a communion in the agony of Christ . . . the identification of our own *agonia* with the *agonia* of the God Who has emptied Himself . . . It is the acceptance of life in the midst of death, not because we have courage, or light, or wisdom to accept, but because by some miracle the God of Life Himself accepts to live, in us, at the very moment we descend into death.[23]

Many trauma survivors have a deep understanding of a sacred world that sustains them. This is not about compensation for the past, nor is it a byproduct of failed early relationships or the self-protective defenses, but Kalsched thinks is rather "an everlasting fact of humankind's experience on the planet and the trauma survivor knows this better than most . . . There are also few, if any, atheists among trauma survivors."[24] Another therapist, Natalie Collins, movingly writes, "My experience as a traumatized person and over a decade of working with traumatized people is that we are some of the most able to know God and to show God to others; indeed, Jesus stated that blessed are those who mourn."[25]

All journeying towards soul recovery and the process of becoming the self we are intended to be involves the psychological and the spiritual, and the journey is heroic. At the beginning of this book the idea of the night sea journey as a universal myth was discussed. It is often a journey toward a spiritual homeland, a place the soul longs for. For the person traumatized as a child the journey starts from a place of despair and uncertainty and travels further into that despair and uncertainty, but gathering wisdom and insight as we go, it is deeply courageous. Paradoxically, it is the soul that calls us into the night sea, and the soul that greets us on the shore as we return. It is this heroic journey that helps makes sense of life. The quest for the soul brings us, as Sellner found,

23. O'Connell, "Hope," 213.

24. Kalsched, *Trauma and the Soul*, 5.

25. Collins, "Broken or Superpowered?," 203.

"face-to-face with my deeper self and with my God . . . I am not the same, and never will be again."[26]

Joe earlier describes Thomas Merton's epiphany in front of the great Buddhist statues in Polonnaruwa. Merton's account includes this sentence: "I have now seen and have pierced through the surface and have got beyond the shadow and the disguise."[27] This could also be a description of soul recovery through night sea journeying. As with Jung, who could emerge from his deep dive into the unconscious with the realization that the soul is a child, and that God in his soul is a child, the divine innocence is once again glimpsed, but this time through the integration of the past troubled experiences. This new glimpse is of a different and deeper innocence, one possible only on the far side of experience—beyond the shadow of the trauma, and beyond the disguises used to cope with what happened: where the past is both witnessed to and transcended. The soul that is recovered is the child of the resurrection, wounded and transformed.

26. Sellner, *Soul-Making*, 159.

27. Merton, *Other Side*, 323.

# Spiritual Practices for the Night Sea Journey

## BREATHING PRACTICES

The breath is the key to feeling grounded, and here are two breathing practices linked to the sea.

### 1. Waves

The body always moves in round movements
there is nothing vertical
movements are like waves
you have to go with them.

each time you breathe in
and each time you breathe out
it's like offering your body to this wave
that runs up and down
up and down
the whole length of your body.[1]

1. Sabatini, *Breath*, 123.

## 2. Ocean pulsation breath

Sit with your eyes closed, relax the eyes and relax the body that's touching the ground. Feel your crown rise upward to the sky.

Turn the palms up—our state of mind is revealed in our hands, when we get stressed, they clench, so help your hands find softness.

The hands extend out to the side as you breathe in through the nose, and the hands come together as you breath out through the mouth. Make a sound like the waves as they reach the shore.

Your hands are like kelp—like seaweed floating and moving in the water as the tide comes in and out. Breathe in to the power of the waves, and out to the shore channeling the ocean's energy.

As you finish this practice bring your hands over the heart.[2]

## 3. In times of spiritual dryness and desolation: just breathe

"Spiritual dryness is indeed inevitable . . . We will be much helped to bear these desert stretches by . . . recognition . . . of the normality and necessity of such desolation." Baron Von Hugel suggests modifying any expectations and any prayers during this time perhaps even to "a few uttered aspirations. And, if the desolation is more acute, we will act somewhat like the Arab caravans behave in the face of a blinding sandstorm in the desert." The people dismount and "throw themselves on their faces in the sand; and there they remain, patient and uncomplaining, till the storm passes and until, with their wonted patient endurance, they can and do continue on their way."[3] In other words, just breathe, until the worst has passed.

2. Adapted from Finn, "Blissology Project Metta".
3. Baron von Hugel, in Phillips, *Choice is Always Ours*, 293.

## MEDITATIONS FOR SOUL RECOVERY

### 1. "Peace, be still" meditation

Simply focus on your breath as you breathe normally. Thank God for each breath, then start to repeat a short prayer in your mind. Breathe one word in, and the second part out. If you want to, extend your breaths to be longer and deeper, which can help in times of stress. Use the words Jesus spoke to calm the waves and the storm: breathe in the word "peace," breathe out the phrase "be still."

### 2. Self-acceptance meditation

The purpose of meditation is to try to stop thinking, to empty the mind of all the pressures, including the pressure of meditating well. The spiritual teacher Ram Dass spoke about resting our weary minds, and the minds of those surviving a traumatic childhood are at times old and weary beyond their years, and need a space to rest.

The idea of self-acceptance is to sit with who one is, and how one is at the moment—to sit without wishing that things were different. This includes accepting what may be happening in the mind and knowing that while thoughts and emotions arise, they also disappear, to be replaced by another thought, or another emotion, or another feeling, or sensation. Breathe in: "I accept who I am." Breathe out: "God loves me for who I am."

### 3. Meditation to aid the struggle of moving from feeling stuck towards growing in creativity

Look back on the day:

How many opportunities were there today where I had to make a decision?

Was it really possible to choose?

How many times did I make a decision on what I thought others wanted, or what I thought I "ought" to do?

When did the creative part of me emerge, rather than being taken over by old habits or autonomous behavior?

Can I congratulate myself when I felt good and happy about a decision that I made?

### 4. Meditation to open to a deeper sense of divine consciousness

This meditation can happen at any time of the day or night. It involves opening oneself to allow a sense of spacious awareness, and letting the transcendent spirit become immanent. Perhaps use the image of the sky, the vast sky that stretches across one's mind with infinite depth and infinite space. Anything that comes into the mind are like small clouds that don't change the sky as they drift across. Open to the vastness that is within and feel that you are part of the divine presence, feel part of something that is eternal—"Giving the depth of one's being to that whose depth has no end." Try this: "I say inwardly on the intake of breath: 'I breathe your blue sky deeply in,' then on the exhale, 'To blow it gladly back again.'" And: "I breathe the resurrection power in . . . to vibrate in me through and through." [4]

## PRAYER

### 1. A Prayer of unknowing

> My Lord God, I have no idea where I am going. I do not see the road ahead of me. I cannot know for certain where it will end. Nor do I really know myself, and the fact that I think I am following Your will does not mean that I am actually doing so. But I believe that the desire to please You does in fact please You. And I hope I have

4. Phillips, *Choice is Always Ours*, 263.

that desire in all that I am doing. I hope that I will never do anything apart from that desire. And I know that, if I do this, You will lead me by the right road, though I may know nothing about it. Therefore I will trust You always though I may seem to be lost and in the shadow of death. I will not fear, for You are ever with me, and You will never leave me to face my perils alone. Amen.[5]

## 2. God as our guide

"Be a bright flame before me. Oh God, a guiding star above me.
Be a smooth path below me, a kindly shepherd behind me, tonight and forever.
Alone with none, but you, my God I journey on my way;
what need I fear when you are near, O Lord of night and day?
More secure am I when in your hand than if a multitude did round me stand."[6]

## 3. Holding tight

This is a prayer Harriet Tubman recited regularly when she led runaway slaves to freedom in the North:

"I'm going to hold steady on You. You've got to see me through."[7]

## 4. A psalm of thanks

"Return, O my soul, to your rest'
for the Lord has dealt bountifully with you.
For you have delivered my soul from death,
my eyes from tears,
my feet from stumbling.
I walk before the Lord
in the land of the living."[8]

5. Merton, *Thoughts in Solitude*, 79.
6. Hillyard-Parker, ed., *Stories of Encounter*, 122.
7. Tubman, in Hill, *Dangerous Prayers*, 179.
8. Psalm 116:7–9.

# Bibliography


Arden, Margaret. *Midwifery of the Soul.* London: Free Association, 1998.

Arel, Stephanie N. *Affect Theory, Shame and Christian Formation.* London: Palgrave Macmillan, 2016.

———. *Bearing Witness: The Wounds of Mass Trauma at Memorial Museums.* Minneapolis: Fortress, 2023.

Baring, Anne. *The Dream of the Cosmos.* Dorset, UK: Archive, 2013.

Bond, H. Lawrence, ed. *Nicholas of Cusa: Selected Spiritual Writings.* Mahwah, NJ: Paulist, 1997.

Brock, Rita Nakashima, and Rebecca Ann Parker. *Proverbs of Ashes.* Boston: Beacon, 2001.

Campbell, Joseph. "Ep. 1: Joseph Campbell and the Power of Myth — 'The Hero's Adventure.'" Moyers: Explore the Bill Moyers Collection at the Library of Congress, June 21, 1988. https://billmoyers.com/content/ep-1-joseph-campbell-and-the-power-of-myth-the-hero%E2%80%99s-adventure-audio/.

Carson, Rachel. "Undersea." *Atlantic Monthly* 78 (1937) 55–67.

Catherine of Siena. *The Dialogue of the Seraphic Virgin, Catherine of Siena.* Translated by Algar Thorold. London: Kegan Paul, Trench, Trubner, 1896.

Chiffolo, Anthony F., ed. *At Prayer with the Saints.* Liguori, MO: Liguori, 1998.

Collins, Natalie. "Broken or Superpowered? Traumatized People, Toxic Doublethink and the Healing Potential of Evangelical Christian Communities." In *Feminist Trauma Theologies: Body, Scripture and Church in Critical Perspective*, edited by Karen O'Donnell and Katie Cross, 195–225. London: SCM, 2020.

Crum, J. M. C. "Love Is Come Again." Hymnary.org, https://hymnary.org/text/now_the_green_blade_riseth.

Depressed Anonymous. "12 Steps of Depressed Anonymous." https://depressedanonymous.org/fellowship/12-steps-of-depressed-anonymous/.

Downton, James V., Jr. *Night Sea Journey: The Ordeal of Individuation.* Self-published, 2018.

Dunne, John, S. *A Search for God in Time and Memory.* Notre Dame: University of Notre Dame Press, 1977.

Epstein, Helen. *The Long Half-Lives of Love and Trauma.* Lexington, MA: Plunkett Lake, 2018.

Fauteux, Kevin. *The Recovery of the Self, Regression and Redemption in Religious Experience.* New York: Paulist, 1994.

Finley, James. *The Healing Path.* Maryknoll, NY: Orbis, 2023.

Finn, Eoin. "Blissology Project Metta-Physical Yoga (37 Mins)." YouTube video, 37:37. https://www.youtube.com/watch?v=l-AFATvAo2k.

Firman, John, and Ann Gila. *The Primal Wound.* New York: State University of New York Press, 1997.

Freud, Anna. "Identification with the Aggressor." In *The Ego and the Mechanisms of Defence*, 117–31. London: Hogarth Press and the Institute of Psychoanalysis, 1961.

Freud, Sigmund. *Beyond the Pleasure Principle, Standard Edition XVIII.* London: Hogarth Press and the Institute of Psychoanalysis, 1955.

———. "Repression." In *On the History of the Psycho-Analytic Movement, Standard Edition XIV*, 146–58. London: Hogarth Press and the Institute of Psychoanalysis, 1957.

Gardner, Fiona. *The Only Mind Worth Having.* Eugene, OR: Cascade, 2015.

Geyer, John B. "The Night of Dumah, (Isaiah XXI 11–12)." *Vetus Testamentum* 42 (1992) 317–39.

Goudge, Elizabeth. *The Scent of Water.* Peabody, MA: Hendrickson, [1963] 2011.

Greenlee, Harold, J. "More than These? John 21:15." *Journal of Translation* 1 (2005) 19–20.

Grotstein, James. *Who is the Dreamer, Who Dreams the Dream.* Hillsdale, NJ: Analytic, 2000.

Guntrip, Harry. *Personal Relations Therapy: The Collected Papers of H.J.S. Guntrip.* Edited by Jeremy Hazell. Northvale, NJ: Jason Aronson, 1994.

Herman, Judith. *Trauma and Recovery.* New York: Basic, 1992.

Hill, Susan. *Dangerous Prayers: 50 Powerful Prayers that Changed the World.* Nashville: Thomas Nelson, 2019.

Hillyard-Parker, Hugh, ed. *Stories of Encounter, Pray Now Devotions, Reflections, Blessings and Prayer Activities.* Wells, UK: St Andrews, 2017.

Ibsen, Henrik. *John Gabriel Borkman.* In *The Master Builder and Other Plays*, edited by Betty Radice and Robert Baldrick, 285–376. London: Penguin, 1958.

Johnson, Maxwell, E., ed. *Benedictine Daily Prayer: A Short Breviary.* Collegeville, MN: Liturgical, 2015.

Julian of Norwich. *Revelations of Divine Love.* London: Hodder and Stoughton, 1987.

Jung, Carl. "Answer to Job." In *Psychology and Religion: West and East, The Collected Works of C. G. Jung, Volume 11*, 355–476. London: Kegan Paul, 1958.

———. *The Archetypes and the Collective Unconscious: The Collected Works of C. G. Jung, Volume 9, Part 1.* London: Routledge and Kegan Paul, 1959.

———. *The Integration of the Personality.* London: Kegan Paul, Trench, Trubner, 1946.

———. *C. G. Jung, Letters, Volume 1*. London: Routledge and Kegan Paul, 1973.
———. *C. G. Jung, Letters, Volume 2*. London: Routledge and Kegan Paul, 1976.
———. *Memories, Dreams and Reflections*. London: Collins, Fount, 1963.
———. *Mysterium Coniunctionis: The Collected Works of C. G. Jung, Volume 14*. London: Routledge and Kegan Paul, 1963.
———. *The Practice of Psychotherapy: The Collected Works of C. G. Jung, Volume 16*. Princeton, NJ: Bollingen Foundation: Princeton University Press, 1954.
———. *Psychology and Religion, West and East: The Collected Works of C. G. Jung, Volume 11*. London: Routledge and Kegan Paul, 1958.
———. *The Red Book: Liber Novus*. Edited by S. Shamdasani. New York: W. W. Norton, 2009.
———. *Symbols of Transformation: The Collected Works of C. G. Jung, Volume 5*. London: Routledge and Kegan Paul, 1956.
Kalsched, Donald. *Trauma and the Soul*. London: Routledge, 2013.
Lane, Belden C. "Christ's Descent into Hell, Hadewijch, and the Fierceness of Love: A Spirituality of Holy Saturday." *Spiritus* 23 (2023) 146–54.
Carey, Benedict. "Expert on Mental Illness Reveals Her Own Fight." *New York Times*, June 23, 2011. https://www.nytimes.com/2011/06/23/health/23lives.html?_r=2&emc=eta1.
Malbon, Elizabeth Struthers. *Narrative Space and Mythic Meaning in Mark*. Sheffield: Sheffield Academic, 1991.
McGann, Diarmuid. *The Journeying Self*. Mahwah, NJ: Paulist, 1985. .
———. *Journeying within Transcendence*. London: Collins, 1989.
Merton, Thomas. *Contemplative Prayer*. London: Darton, Longman and Todd, 1973.
———. *Entering the Silence: The Journals of Thomas Merton, Volume 2*. Edited by Jonathan Montaldo. New York: HarperCollins, 1997.
———. "Herakleitos the Obscure." In *A Thomas Merton Reader*, edited by Thomas P. McDonnell, 258–71. New York: Image Doubleday, 1974.
———. *The Inner Experience*. London: SPCK, 2003.
———. *Love and Living*. London: Sheldon, 1979.
———. *No Man Is an Island*. London: Hollis and Carter, 1955.
———. *The Other Side of the Mountain: The Journals of Thomas Merton, Volume 7, 1967–1968*. Edited by Patrick Hart. New York: HarperCollins, 1998.
———. *Run to the Mountain: The Journals of Thomas Merton, Volume 1, 1939–1941*. Edited by Patrick Hart. New York: HarperCollins, 1995.
———. *A Search for Solitude: The Journals of Thomas Merton, Volume 3, 1952–1960*. Edited by Lawrence S. Cunningham. New York: HarperCollins, 1997.
———. *The Seven Storey Mountain*. New York: Harcourt Brace, 1948.
———. *The Sign of Jonas*. London: Hollis and Carter, 1953.
———. *Thoughts in Solitude*. New York: Farrar, Straus and Giroux, 1999.

Mind Map Inspiration. "Riding the Waves of Lifes [*sic*] Ups and Downs." https://mindmapinspiration.com/riding-the-waves-of-lifes-ups-and-downs/.

Morris, David J. *The Evil Hours*. Boston: Mariner, 2016.

Myers, Ched, *Binding the Strong Man, a Political Reading of Mark's Story of Jesus*. Maryknoll, NY: Orbis, 2000.

Neumann, Erich. "On the Moon and Matriarchal Consciousness." *Spring Journal*, Analytical Psychology Club of New York, 1954, 83–100.

O'Connell, Patrick. "Hope." In *The Thomas Merton Encyclopedia*, edited by William H. Shannon et al., 212–14. Maryknoll, NY: Orbis, 2002.

Phillips, Dorothy Berkely. *The Choice is Always Ours*. Wheaton, IL: Re-Quest, 1975.

Plum Village App. "No Mud No Lotus—Short Film with the Words of Thich Nhat Hanh." YouTube video, 2:58. https://www.youtube.com/watch?v=stiG6IzDITc.

Rambo, Shelly. *Resurrecting Wounds: Living in the Afterlife of Trauma*. Waco, TX: Baylor University Press, 2017.

———. *Spirit and Trauma*. Louisville: Westminster John Knox, 2010.

Rodman, F. Robert. *Winnicott*. Cambridge: Da Capo, 2003.

Romero, Oscar. *The Violence of Love*. Compiled and translated by James R. Brockman. Maryknoll, NY: Orbis, 2004.

Sabatini, Sandra. *Breath: The Essence of Yoga*. London: Thorsons, 2000.

Schaverien, Joy. *Boarding School Syndrome: The Psychological Trauma of the 'Privileged' Child*. London: Routledge, 2015.

Sellner, Edward C. *Soul-Making*. Mystic, CT: Twenty-Third, 1991.

———. *Step 5, Telling my Story*. Center City, MN: Hazelden Foundation, 1992.

Shengold, Leonard. *Soul Murder Revisited*. New Haven: Yale University Press, 1999.

Singer, June. *Boundaries of the Soul*. New York: Anchor, 1973.

Tagore, Rabindranath. "On the Seashore." Poetry Foundation, https://www.poetryfoundation.org/poems/45670/on-the-seashore.

Tillich, Paul. *The Courage to Be*. London: Fontana, 1962.

Van der Kolk, Bessel. *The Body Keeps the Score*. London: Penguin, 2015.

Von Franz, Marie. *Dreams*. Boston: Shambala, 1998.

Williams, Harry. *Some Day I'll Find You*. London: Mitchell Beazley, 1982.

———. *True to Experience*. London: Mitchell Beazley, 1984

Wilson, Bill. "Bill W. – Carl Jung Letters How AA History Was Made – Grapevine January 1963." https://gugogs.org/2020/05/14/bill-w-carl-jung-letters-how-aa-history-was-made-grapevine-january-*1963*/.

Winnicott, Donald. "Fear of Breakdown." *The International Review of Psycho-Analysis,1* (1974) 103-7.

———. *The Maturational Processes and the Facilitating Environment*. London: Hogarth Press and the Institute of Psycho-Analysis, 1965.

———. "Primary Maternal Preoccupation." In *Through Paediatrics to Psycho-Analysis*, 300–305. London: Hogarth Press and the Institute of Psycho-Analysis, 1982.

# Index

www.ingramcontent.com/pod-product-compliance
Lightning Source LLC
Chambersburg PA
CBHW020555270326
41927CB00006B/851
* 9 7 9 8 3 8 5 2 2 7 8 3 9 *